ART BOOKS

FROM CRESCENT MOON PUBLISHING

Leonardo da Vinci
by James Pearson

Early Netherlandish Painting
by Rosalind Mutter

Piero della Francesca
by Naomi Haskell

Giovanni Bellini
by Julia Davis

Eric Gill: Nuptials of God
by Anthony Hoyland

Minimal Art and Artists In the 1960s and After
by Laura Garrard

Postwar Art
by George Knighton

Vincent van Gogh: Visionary Landscapes
by Stuart Morris

Max Beckmann
by Stuart Morris

Egon Schiele: Sex and Death in Purple Stockings
by D. Simon Eade

Mark Rothko: The Art of Transcendence
by Julia Davis

Jasper Johns
by L.M. Poole

Brice Marden
by Laura Garrard

Frank Stella: American Abstract Artist
by James Pearson

The Light Eternal: J.M.W. Turner
by Jeremy Mark Robinson

Maurice Sendak and the Art of Children's Book Illustration
by L.M. Poole

Sex in Art: Pornography and Pleasure in Painting and Sculpture
by Cassidy Hughes

Glorification: Religious Abstraction
In Renaissance and 20th Century Painting
by Jeremy Mark Robinson

The Art of Andy Goldsworthy
by William Malpas

Andy Goldsworthy: Touching Nature
by William Malpas

Andy Goldsworthy In Close-Up
by William Malpas

The Art of Richard Long
by William Malpas

Constantin Brancusi: Sculpting the Essence of Things
by James Pearson

Alison Wilding: The Embrace of Sculpture
by Susan Quinnell

The Erotic Object: Sexuality in Sculpture
From Prehistory to the Present Day
by Susan Quinnell

Land Art: A Complete Guide to Landscape, Environmental,
Earthworks, Nature, Sculpture and Installation Art
by William Malpas

Land Art In Close-Up
by William Malpas

Colourfield Painting: Minimal, Cool, Hard Edge, Serial
and Post-Painterly Abstract Art From the Sixties to the Present
by Laura Garrard

TITIAN

TITIAN

ESTELLE M. HURLL

CRESCENT MOON

First published 1902. This edition © 2017.

Printed and bound in the U.S.A.
Set in Book Antiqua 10 on 14pt.
Designed by Radiance Graphics.

Thanks to the authors and publishers quoted.

British Library Cataloguing in Publication data

ISBN-13 97818617166088

CRESCENT MOON PUBLISHING
P.O. Box 1312, Maidstone, Kent, ME14 5XU
Great Britain, www.crmoon.com

CONTENTS

NOTE ON THE TEXT

The text is from *Titian: A Collection of Fifteen Pictures and a Portrait of the Painter With Introduction and Interpretation* by Estelle Hurll, published by Houghton, Mifflin & Co., 1901, part of the Riverside Art Series.

The format of the book was based around fifteen artworks. They are included in the illustrations section, along with many other works.

Footnotes are in square brackets, thus: [1].

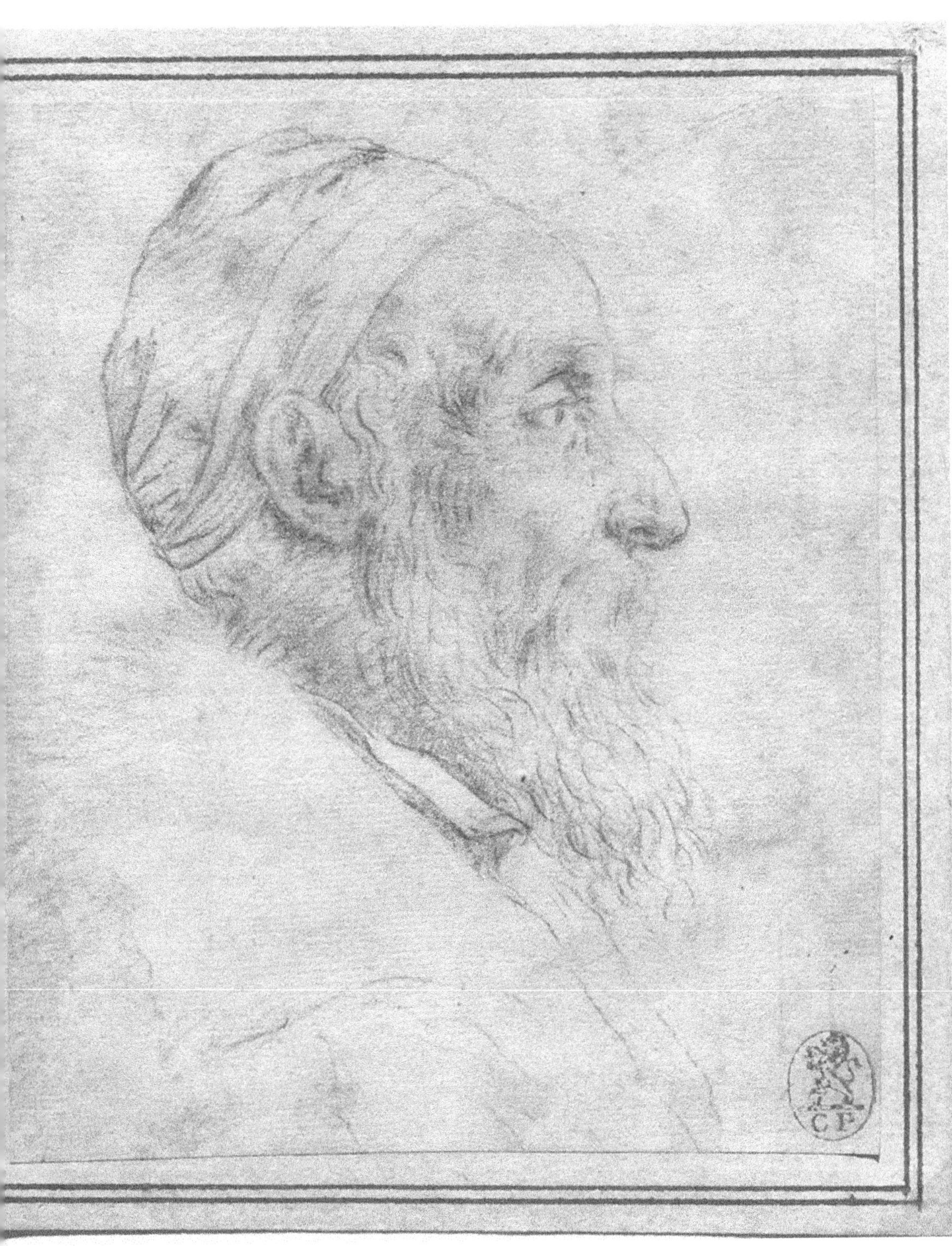

Titian, Self-Portrait

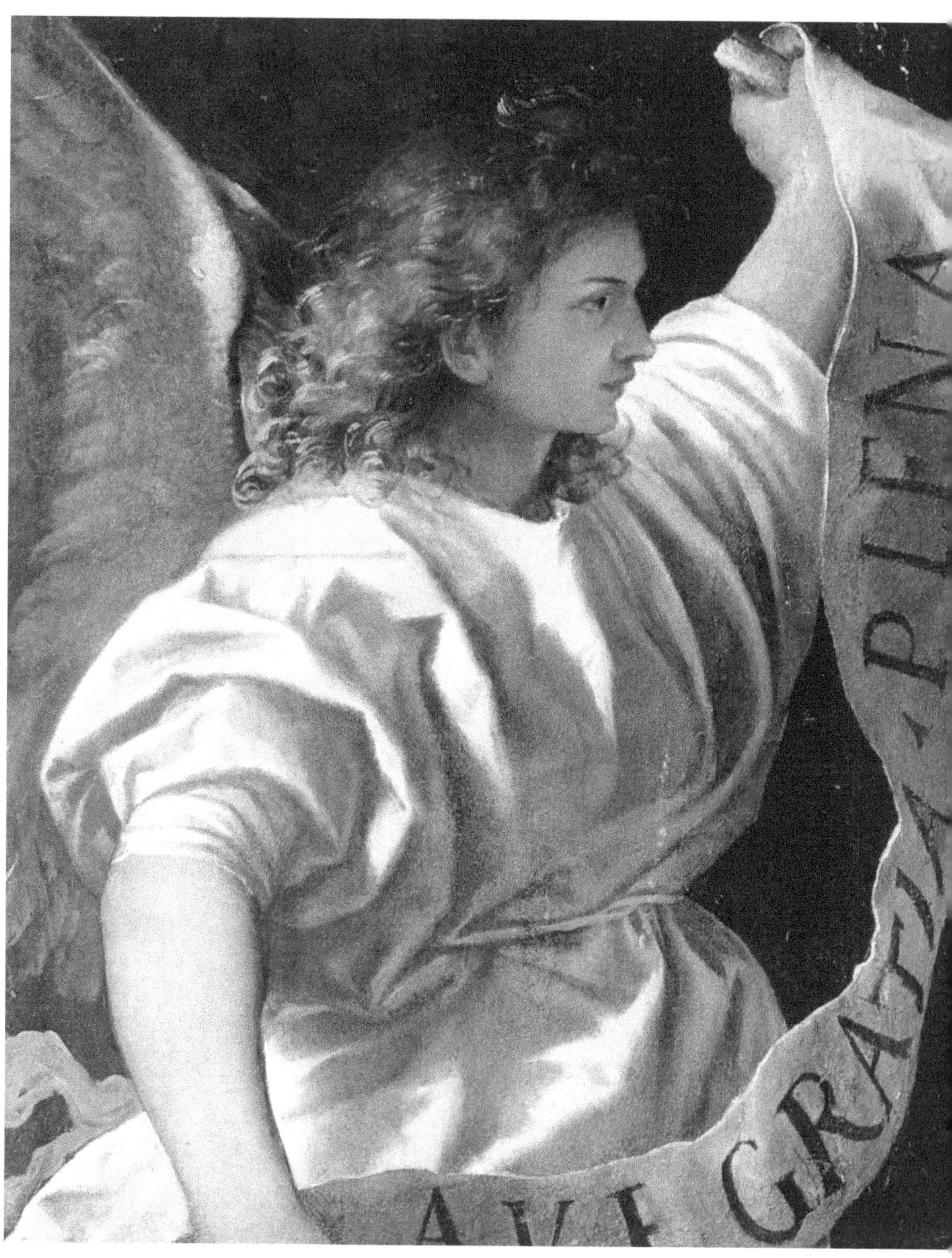

Titian, Annunciation, 1522, detail

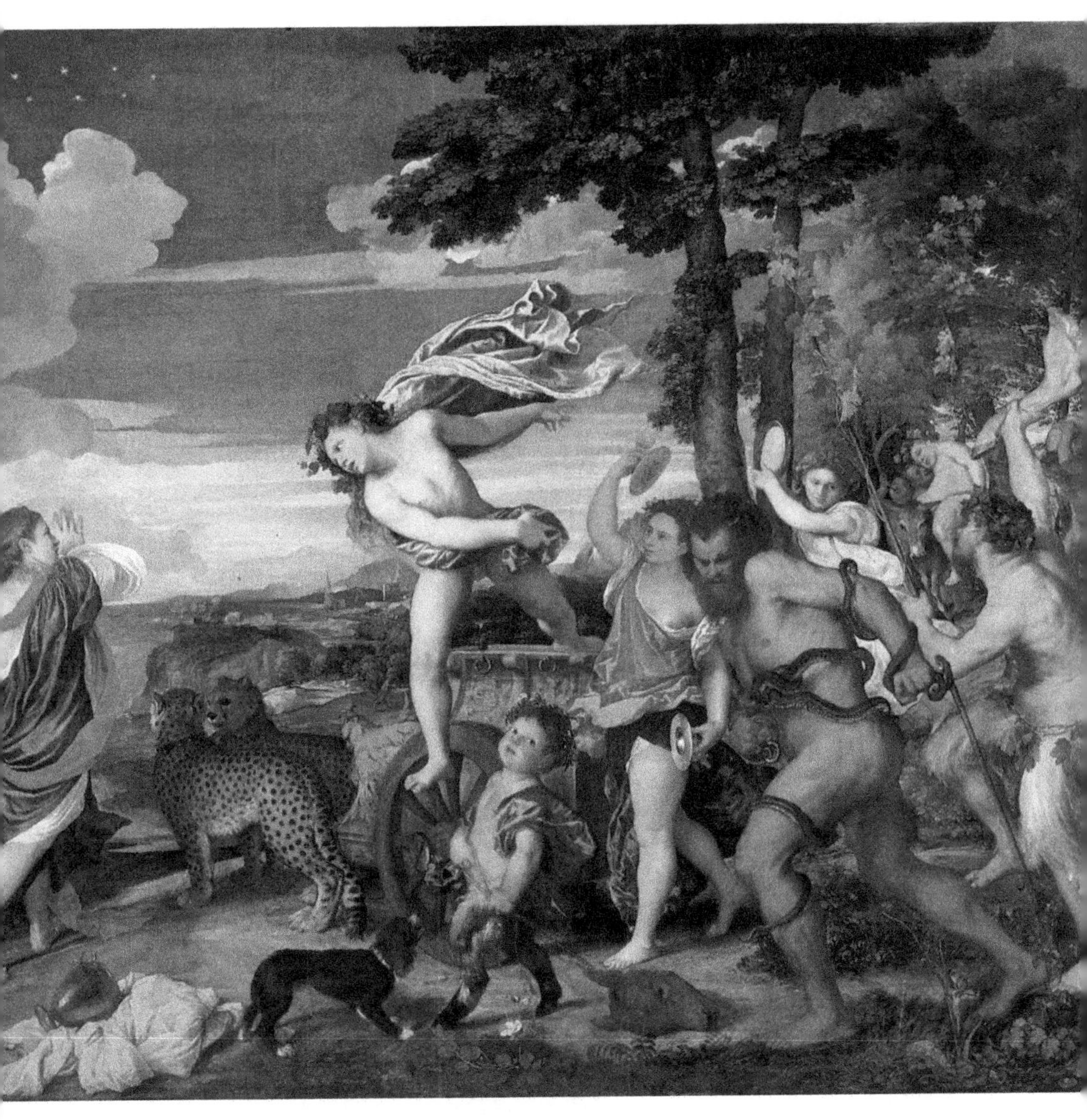

Titian, Bacchus and Ariadne, 1520-23, London

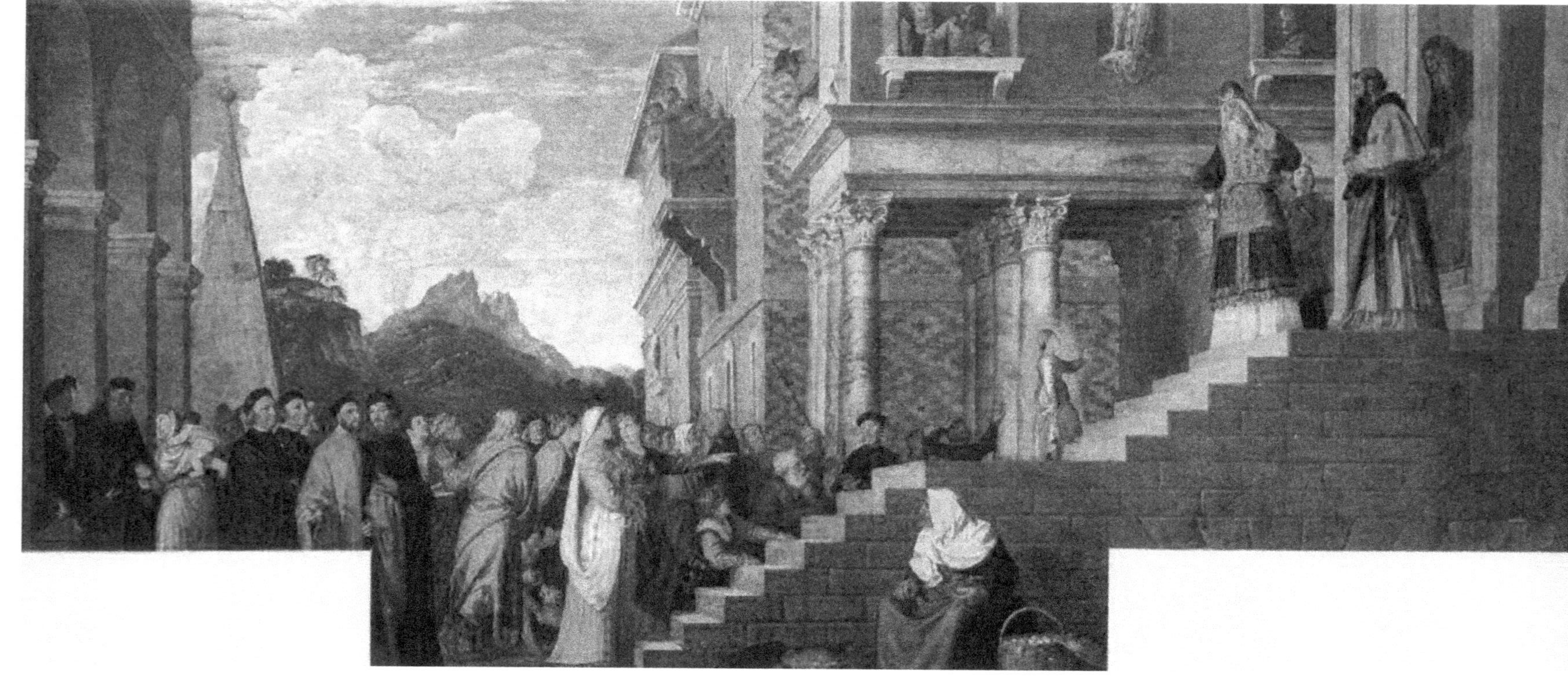

Titian, The Presentation of the Virgin, 1534-38

PREFACE

To give proper variety to this little collection, the selections are equally divided between portraits and "subject" pictures of religious or legendary character.

The Flora, the Bella and the Philip II. show the painter's most characteristic work in portraiture, while the Pesaro Madonna, the Assumption, and the Christ of the Tribute Money stand for his highest achievement in sacred art.

ESTELLE M. HURLL.

New Bedford, Mass.
March, 1901.

INTRODUCTION

I

ON TITIAN'S CHARACTER AS AN ARTIST

"There is no greater name in Italian art - therefore no greater in art - than that of Titian." These words of the distinguished art critic, Claude Phillips, express the verdict of more than three centuries. It is agreed that no other painter ever united in himself so many qualities of artistic merit. Other painters may have equalled him in particular respects, but "rounded completeness," quoting another critic's phrase, is "what stamps Titian as a master." [1]

To begin with the qualities which are apparent even in black and white reproduction, we are impressed at once with the vitality which informs all his figures. They are breathing human beings, of real flesh and blood, pulsing with life. They represent all classes and conditions, from such royal sitters as Charles V. and Philip II. to the peasants and boatmen who served as models for St. Christopher, St. John, and the Pharisee of the Tribute Money. They portray, too, every age: the tender infancy of the Christ child, the girlhood of the Virgin, the dawning manhood of the Man with the Glove, the maidenhood of Medea, the young motherhood of Mary, the virile middle life of Venetian Senators, the noble old age of St. Jerome and St. Peter, each is set vividly before us.

The list contains no mystics and ascetics: life, and life abundant, is the keynote of Titian's art. The abnormal finds no place in it. Health and happiness are to him interchangeable terms.

Yet it must not be supposed that Titian's delineation of life stopped short with the physical: he was besides a remarkable interpreter of the inner life. Though not as profound a psychologist as Leonardo or Lotto, he had at all times a just appreciation of character, and, on occasion, rose to a supreme touch in its interpretation. In such studies as the Flora, where he is interested chiefly in working out certain technical problems, he takes small pains to make anything more of his subject than a beautiful animal. The Man with the Glove stands at the other end of the scale. Here we have a personality so individual, and so possessing, as it were, that the portrait takes rank among the world's masterpieces of psychic interpretation.

In his best works Titian's sense of the dramatic holds the golden mean between conventionality and sensationalism. In the group of sacred personages surrounding the Madonna and Child there is sufficient action to constitute a reason for their presence, - to relieve the figures of that artificial and purely spectacular character which they have in the earlier art, - yet the action is restrained and dignified as befits the occasion. The pose of both figures in the Christ of the Tribute Money is in the highest degree dramatic without being in any way theatrical. The tempered dignity of Titian's dramatic power is also admirably seen in the Assumption of the Virgin. The apostles' action is full of passion, yet without violence; the buoyant motion of the Virgin is unmarred by any exaggeration.

The same painting illustrates Titian's magnificent mastery of composition. Perhaps the Pesaro Madonna alone of all his other works is worthy to be classed with it in this respect. It is impossible to conceive of anything better in composition than these two works. Not a line in either could be altered without detriment to the organic unity of the plan.

The crowning excellence of Titian is his color. The chief of the school in which color was the characteristic quality, he represents all the best elements in its color work. If others excelled him in single efforts or in some one respect, none equalled him for sustained grandeur. A recent criticism sums up his color qualities succinctly in these words: "He had at once enough of golden strength, enough of depth, enough of éclat; his color, profound and powerful *per se*, impresses us more than that of the others, because he brought more of other qualities to enforce it." [2]

Titian's works easily fall into a few groups, according to the subject treated. In mythological themes he was in his natural element. Here he could express the sheer joy of living which was common to the Venetian and the Greek. Here physical beauty was its own excuse for being, without recourse to any ulterior significance. Here he could exercise unhindered his marvellous skill in modelling the human form along those perfect lines of grace which give Greek sculpture its distinctive character. It is in his earlier period that his affinity with the Greek spirit is closest, and we see it in perfect fruition in the Medea and Venus.

Titian's treatment of sacred subjects is in the diverse moods of his many-sided artistic nature. The great ceremonial altar pieces, such as the Assumption of the Virgin, and the Pesaro Madonna, are a perfect reflection of the religious spirit of his environment. Religion was with the Venetians a delightful pastime, an occasion for festivals and pageants, a means of increasing the civic glory. These great decorative pictures are full of the pomp and magnificence dear to Venice, full of the joy and pride of life.

Yet in another mood Titian paints the life of the Holy Family as a pastoral idyl. A sunny landscape, a happy young mother, a laughing baby boy, bring the sacred subject very near to common human sympathies.

Some of Titian's professedly sacred pictures are in the vein of pure *genre*, painted in a period when this department of art had not yet attained independent existence. We see such works in the St. Christopher and the St. John. These direct studies of the people throw an interesting light upon the painter of ideal beauty: they show an otherwise unsuspected vigor.

The Christ of the Tribute Money stands alone in Titian's sacred art. The technical qualities are thoroughly characteristic of his hand, but a new note is struck in spiritual feeling. Virile, without coarseness; gentle, without weakness, the chief figure is perhaps the most intellectual ideal of Christ which has been conceived in art.

Titian's landscapes, though holding an accessory place only in his art, are counted by the critical art historian with those of Giorgione, as the practical beginning of this branch of art. He knew how to express "the quintessence of nature's most significant beauties without a too slavish adherence to any special set of natural facts." [3] His imagination interpreted many of nature's moods, from the pastoral calm environing Medea and Venus to the stormy grandeur of the forest in which St. Peter Martyr met his fate.

It is undoubtedly as a portrait-painter that Titian's many great qualities meet in their utmost perfection. His feeling for textures, the delicacy with which he painted the hair and the hands; his skill in modelling; his instinct for pose; the infinite variety of his resources, made an incomparable equipment in the secondary matters of portrait painting. To these he added, as we have seen, the two highest essentials of the art, the power of giving life to his sitter, and the gift of insight into character.

Nature made him a court painter; he loved to impart to his sitter that air of noble distinction whose secret he so well understood. Yet he was too large a man to let this or any other natural preference hamper him. Something of himself, it is true, he frequently put into his figures, yet he was at times capable of thoroughly objective work. He stands perhaps somewhere between the extreme subjectivity of Van Dyck and the splendid realism of Velasquez. The noble company of his sitters, emperors, kings, doges, popes, cardinals and bishops, noblemen, poets and beautiful women, still make their presence felt in the world. Theirs was a deathless fame on whom the painter conferred the gift of his art.

Titian's temperament was keenly sensitive to the influences of his environment, and in his extraordinary length of days, Venice passed through various changes, political, social, artistic and religious, which left their mark upon his work. One cannot make a random selection from his pictures and pronounce upon the qualities of his art. The work of his youth, his maturity, his old age, has each a character of its own. It is this rounding out of his art life through successive stages of growth and even of decay that gives the entire body of his works the character of a living organism.

II

ON BOOKS OF REFERENCE

The original source of biographical material relating to Titian is in Vasari's "Lives of the Painters," the best edition of which is the Foster translation, annotated with critical and explanatory comments by E. H. and E. W. Blashfield and A. A. Hopkins. The most complete modern biography is that by Crowe and Cavalcaselle, in two large volumes (published in 1877), but as this is now out of print, it can be consulted only in the large libraries. Some of the conclusions of these writers have been challenged by later critics, Morelli and others, and should not be accepted without weighing the new arguments. The volume on "Titian: A Study of his Life and Work," by Claude Phillips, Keeper of the Wallace Collection, London, is in line with the modern methods of criticism, and is written in a delightful vein of appreciation. The two parts of the book, The Earlier Work and The Later Work, correspond to the two monographs for "The Portfolio," in which the work was first published.

In the general histories of Italian art, valuable chapters on Titian are contained in Kugler's "Handbook of the Italian Schools" (to be read in the latest edition by A. H. Layard) and Mrs. Jameson's "Early Italian Painters" (to be read in the latest revision by Estelle M. Hurll). A monograph on Titian is issued in the German Series of Art Monographs, edited by H. Knackfuss.

Interesting suggestions upon the study of Titian's art will be found in the following references: In Mrs. Oliphant's "Makers of Venice;" in Berenson's "Venetian Painters of the Renaissance;" in Symonds's volume on Fine Arts in the series "Renaissance in Italy." Burckhardt's "Cicerone" has some valuable pages on Titian, but the book is out of print. A List of Titian's work is given in Berenson's "Venetian Painters."

III

HISTORICAL DIRECTORY OF THE PICTURES OF THIS COLLECTION

Portrait frontispiece. Probably the portrait mentioned by Vasari as painted in 1502. In the Prado Gallery, Madrid. Size: 2 ft. 10 in. by 2 ft. 1? in.

1. *The Physician Parma.* It appears that there is no direct testimony to prove the authorship of this picture, the attribution to Titian having been made by an early director of the gallery, following certain evidence from Rudolfi. Herr Wickhoff claims the picture for Domenico Campagnola, and the recent biographer of Giorgione (Herbert Cook) includes it among the works of that painter. The attribution to Titian is, however, not disputed by the two severest of modern critics, Morelli and Berenson. In the Vienna Gallery. Size: 3 ft. 6 in. by 2 ft. 7 in.

2. *The Presentation of the Virgin (Detail).* Painted for the brotherhood of S. Maria della Carità, and now in the Venice Academy. Date assigned by Berenson 1540. Size of entire picture: 11 ft. 5 in. by 25 ft. 6? in.

3. *The Empress Isabella.* Probably one of the two pictures

referred to in a letter of 1544 from Titian to Charles V. In the Prado Gallery, Madrid. Size: 3 ft. 10 in. by 3 ft. 2? in.

4. *Madonna and Child with Saints.* An early work in the Vienna Gallery, similar to a picture in the Louvre, to which it is considered superior by Crowe and Cavalcaselle. Called an "atelier repetition" by Claude Phillips. Size: 3 ft. 5 in. by 4 ft. 3 in.

5. *Philip II.* Painted 1550, and now in the Prado Gallery, Madrid. Size: 6 ft. 4 in. by 3 ft. 7? in.

6. *St. Christopher.* Painted in fresco on the wall of the Doge's Palace, Venice, in honor of the arrival of the French army at San Cristoforo (near Milan), 1523. Ordered by the doge Andrea Gritti, who was a partisan of the French.

7. *Lavinia.* Painted about 1550, and now in the Berlin Gallery. Size: 3 ft. 3? in. by 2 ft. 7? in.

8. *Christ of the Tribute Money.* According to Vasari, painted for Duke Alfonso of Ferrara in 1514 for door of a press. Assigned by Crowe and Cavalcaselle to the year 1518, the date accepted by Morelli. In the Dresden Gallery. Size: 2 ft. 5? in. by 1 ft. 10 in.

9. *The Bella.* Painted about 1535. In the Pitti Gallery, Florence. Size: 3 ft. 3? in. by 2 ft. 6 in.

10. *Medea and Venus.* Date unknown, but fixed approximately by Morelli between 1510 and 1512. In the Borghese Gallery, Rome. Size: 3 ft. 5 in. by 8 ft. 8 in.

11. *The Man with the Glove.* Assigned to Titian's middle period. In the Louvre, Paris. Size: 3 ft. 31/3 in. by 2 ft. 11 in.

12. *The Assumption of the Virgin (Detail).* Ordered 1516 for high

altar of S. Maria Gloriosa de' Frari, Venice. Shown to public, March 20, 1518. Now in the Venice Academy. Size: 22 ft. 9 in. by 11 ft. 10? in.

13. *Flora.* Painted after 1523. In the Uffizi Gallery, Florence. Size: 3 ft. 8? in. by 3 ft. 1? in.

14. *The Pesaro Madonna.* Finished in 1526 after being seven years in process. Still in original place in the Church of the Frari, Venice.

15. *St. John the Baptist.* Painted in 1556. In the Venice Academy. Size: 6 ft. 5 in. by 4 ft. 5 in.

IV

OUTLINE TABLE OF THE PRINCIPAL EVENTS IN TITIAN'S LIFE[4]

1477.

Titian born at Cadore in the Friuli, north of Venice.

Circa 1488. Removal to Venice.

Bet. 1507-1508. Work on frescoes of Fondaca de' Tedeschi with Giorgione.

1511.

In Padua and Vicenza. Frescoes in the Scuola del Santo, Padua.

Circa 1512. Marriage.

1516.

Assumption of the Virgin begun for the Church of the Frari, Venice.

Titian's first connection with Alfonso I. and the Court of Ferrara.

1518.

Assumption finished.

1519.

Visit in Ferrara, and the Bacchanal, now in the Madrid Gallery.

1522.

Altarpiece for Brescia, and short visit there.

1523.

Visits at Mantua and Ferrara.

1524.

Visit in Ferrara.

Circa 1525. Birth of Titian's son Pomponio.

1526.

Pesaro Madonna.

1528.

Visit in Ferrara.

1530.

Visit in Bologna.

St. Peter Martyr delivered April 27, for Church of SS. Giovanni e Paolo, Venice.

Death of Titian's wife.

1531.

Visit in Ferrara.

Removal from town to suburban residence in Biri.

1532.

Summons to court of Charles V. at Bologna. Portraits of the

Emperor.

1536.
With the Emperor at Astic.

1537.
Portraits of Duke and Duchess of Urbino and the Battle of Cadore. Paintings in Hall of Council of Venice (destroyed by fire 1577).

1540.
Visit to Mantua to attend the funeral of patron Duke Federico Gonzaga.

1541.
Appointment with Emperor at Milan.

1543.
Guest of Cardinal Farnese at Ferrara and Brussels.
Portraits of Cardinal Farnese and Pope Paul III.

1544.
Two portraits of the dead Empress Isabella sent to Charles V.

1545.
Visit to Rome, and portraits of Paul III. and his grandsons.

1546.
Departure from Rome, visit to Florence and return to Venice.

1547.
Completion of altarpiece of Serravalle.

1548.
Journey to Augsburg to meet Charles V., and equestrian

portrait of the Emperor.

To Milan to meet Prince Philip and Duke of Alva. Portrait of Alva.

1549.

Purchase of the house at Biri, formerly rented.

1550.

Visit to court at Augsburg, and portraits of Philip II.

1554.

Pictures completed and sent to Charles V. and Philip II. in Spain: The Virgin Lamenting, the Trinity, the Danaë.

Venus and Adonis sent to London to Philip upon marriage with Mary Tudor.

1555.

Marriage of Titian's daughter Lavinia.

Perseus and Andromeda sent to King Philip.

1556.

St. John the Baptist, painted for S. Maria Maggiore.

1559.

Entombment sent to Philip.

1562.

Christ in the Garden, and the Europa. Last Supper begun.

1563.

Visit to Brescia.

1565.

Visit to Cadore, and plans for frescoes in the Pieve church.

1567.
Martyrdom of St. Lawrence, and a Venus sent to Madrid.

1572.
Visit from Cardinals Granvelle and Pacheco.

1574.
Visit from Henry III. of France.
Allegory of Lepanto finished for Philip II.

1575.
Pieta begun.

1576.
Death of Titian from plague at Venice.

V

SOME OF TITIAN'S CONTEMPORARIES

RULERS.

Emperors:–

Maximilian I. of Germany, 1493-1519.

Charles V. of Germany (I. of Spain) crowned Holy Roman Emperor, 1520. Died 1558.

Kings:–

Philip II. son and successor of Charles V., accession, 1556; death, 1598.

Henry VIII. of England, reigned 1509-1547.

Edward VI. " " 1547-1553.

Mary Tudor " " 1553-1558.

Elizabeth " " 1558-1603.

Francis I. " " 1515-1547.

Henry II. " " 1547-1559.

Catherine de' Medici real ruler of France in reigns of Francis II. and Charles IX., 1559-1574.

Popes:-

Sixtus IV., 1471.Paul III., 1534.
Innocent VIII., 1485.Julius III., 1550.
Alexander VI., 1492.Marcellus II., 1555.
Pius III., 1503.Paul IV., 1555.
Julius II., 1503.Pius IV., 1559.
Leo N., 1513.Pius V., 1566.
Adrian VI., 1522.Gregory XIII., 1572.
Clement VII., 1523.

Doges of Venice:-

Giov. Mocenigo, 1478.Francesco Donato, 1545.
Marco Barbarigo, 1485.Marco Trevisan, 1553.
Agostino Barbarigo, 1486.Francesco Venier, 1554.
Leonardo Loredan, 1501.Lorenzo Priuli, 1556.
Antonio Grimani, 1521.Girolamo Priuli, 1559.
Andrea Gritti, 1523.Pietro Loredan, 1567.
Pietro Lando, 1528.Alvise Mocenigo I., 1570.

Painters:-

Giovanni Bellini, 1428-1516.
Perugino, 1446-1523.
Leonardo da Vinci, 1452-1519.
Michelangelo, 1475-1564.
Bazzi (II Sodoma), 1477-1549.
Giorgione, 1477-1510.

Palma Vecchio, 1480-1528.
Raphael, 1483-1520.
Sebastian del Piombo, 1485-1547.
Andrea del Sarto, 1486-1531.
Correggio, 1494-1534.
Giorgio Vasari, 1512-1574.
Tintoretto, 1518-1594.
Paolo Veronese, 1528-1588.

Men of Letters:–

Ariosto, 1474-1533, poet.
Aretino, 1492-1557, poet.
Tasso, 1544-1595, poet.
Pietro Bembo, 1470-1547, cardinal and master of Latin style.
Jacopo Sadoleto, 1477-1547, cardinal and writer of Latin verses.
Baldassare Castiglione, 1478-1529, diplomatist and scholar.
Aldo Manuzio, 1450-1515, printer; established press at Venice, 1490.
Guicciardini, 1483-1540, historian.

I

THE PHYSICIAN PARMA

We are about to study a few pictures reproduced from the works of a great Venetian painter of the sixteenth century, - Titian. The span of this man's life covered nearly a hundred years, from 1477 to 1576, a period when Venice was a rich and powerful city. The Venetians were a pleasure-loving people, fond of pomp and display. They delighted in sumptuous entertainments, and were particularly given to pageants. We read of the picturesque processions that paraded the square of St. Mark's, or floated in gondolas along the grand canal. The city was full of fine buildings, palaces, churches, and public halls. Their richly ornamented fronts of colored marbles, bordering the blue water of the canals, made a brilliant panorama of color. The buildings were no less beautiful within than without, being filled with the splendid paintings of the Venetian masters.

The pictures in the churches and monasteries illustrated sacred story and the fives of the saints; those in the public halls depicted historical and allegorical themes, while the private palaces were adorned with mythological scenes and portraits.

Titian engaged in works of all these kinds, and seemed equally skilful in each. The great number and variety of his pictures bring vividly before us the manners and customs of his times. His art is like a great mirror in which Venice of the sixteenth century is clearly reflected in all her magnificence. As we study our little prints, we must bear in mind that the original paintings glow with rich and harmonious color. As far as possible let us try to supply this lost color from our imagination.

Nearly all the notable personages of the time sat to Titian for their portraits, - emperors, queens, and princes, popes, and cardinals, the doges, or dukes, of Venice, noblemen, poets, and fair women. Wearing the costumes of a bygone age, these men and women look out of their canvases as if they were still living, breathing human beings. The painter endowed them with the magic gift of immortality. Though the names of many of the sitters are now forgotten, and we know little or nothing of their lives, they are still real persons to us, with their life history written on their faces.

Such is the man called Parma, who is believed to have been a physician of Titian's time, but whose only biography is this portrait. If we were told that it was the portrait of some eminent physician now practising in New York or London, we should perhaps be equally ready to believe it. We might meet such a figure in our streets to-morrow. There is nothing in the costume to mark it as peculiar to any century or country. The black gown is such as is still worn by clergymen and university men. The man would not have to be pointed out to us as a celebrity; we should know him at once as a person of distinction.

The science of medicine was making great progress during the sixteenth century. It was then that the subject of anatomy was first developed by the celebrated Fleming, Vesalius, court physician to Charles V. [5] In this period, also, the science of chemistry first came to be separated from alchemy, and progressive physicians applied the new learning to their practice.

We may be sure that our Doctor Parma belonged to the most enlightened class of his profession. His strong: intellectual face shows him to be one who would have little patience with quackery or superstition. He has a high, noble forehead, keen, penetrating eyes, and a firm mouth. His beautiful white hair gives him a venerable aspect, though he is not of great age. It blows about his face as fine and light as gossamer. He is an ideal "family physician," of a generation ago. We can imagine how children would learn to look upon him with love and respect, perhaps also with a little wholesome fear.

The hand which holds the folds of the long, black gown has a character of its own as definite as that of the face. It is a strong, firm hand, which looks capable of guiding skilfully a surgeon's knife.

Two fine seal rings ornament it. Such rings, sometimes of curious design and workmanship, were often bestowed as gifts by wealthy noblemen upon those who had done them some service.

The doctor Parma looks as good as he is wise. This benign face would grace an assembly of notable clergymen. Indeed, the picture suggests a well-known portrait of the great John Wesley, whose features were cast in the same strong mould, and who also had an abundance of bushy white hair.

By another play of the fancy we could imagine this a portrait of some eminent judge. There is that in the face which indicates the calm, impartial, deliberate mind that belongs to the character. He might now be about to charge the jury, or perhaps even to pronounce sentence.

Still another opinion is that here we have a Venetian senator in his official robes. The man is in any case an ideal professional man, a person of brains and character, who could fill equally well a position of responsibility in medicine, law, administrative affairs, or divinity. With a strict sense of justice, a stern contempt for anything mean and base, and a fatherly tenderness for the weak and oppressed, he is one in whom we could safely put confidence.

II

THE PRESENTATION OF THE VIRGIN

In the town of Nazareth many centuries ago lived a pious old couple, named Joachim and Anna. It is said that they "divided all their substance in three parts: " one part "for the temple," another for "the poor and pilgrims," and the third for themselves. The delight of their old age was their only child Mary, who afterwards became the mother of Jesus. She had been born, as they believed, in answer to their prayers, and they cherished her with peculiar devotion.

That Mary was a good and lovable child beyond common measure we can have no doubt: she was set apart for a strange and holy service. The beautiful story of her early life is told in an old Latin book called the "Legenda Aurea," or the "Golden Legend." This was a collection of old legends written out for the first time by Jacopo de Voragine, an Italian archbishop of the thirteenth century. The early English translation by Caxton, in which we still read the book, preserves the quaint flavor of the original. There is one portion of it describing the dedication, or presentation, of the Virgin in the temple. Before Mary was born, the mother, Anna, had promised the angel of the Lord that she would present the coming child as an offering to the Lord. Long before her day, a certain Hannah had made a like vow under similar circumstances. Her son Samuel, a "child obtained by petition," was "returned," or "lent," to the Lord as long as he lived. [6] A child thus dedicated was early carried to the temple to be educated within its precincts for special service to God.

The presentation of Mary was on this wise: "And then when she had accomplished the time of three years ... they brought her to the temple with offerings. And there was about the temple, after the fifteen psalms of degrees, fifteen steps or grees to ascend up to the temple, because the temple was high set. And nobody might go to the altar of sacrifices that was without, but by the degrees. And then our Lady was set on the lowest step; and mounted up without any help as she had been of perfect age, and when they had performed their offering, they left their daughter in the temple with the other virgins, and they returned into their place. And the Virgin Mary profited every day in all holiness, and was visited daily by angels, and had every day divine visions." [7] We see at once the picture there is in the story, the little girl ascending alone the long flight of steps, with the fond parents gazing after her in wonder. Many artists have put the subject on canvas, and among them our Venetian painter Titian. His is an immense picture, from which the central figure only is reproduced in our illustration.

We must imagine ourselves standing with a great throng of people in the public square in front of the temple. Men, women and children jostle one another near the steps. The old man Joachim and his wife Anna are easily singled out among the number. The windows of the adjoining palaces are full of faces looking into the square. A group of senators stand somewhat apart, looking on. An old peasant woman with a basket of eggs sits in the shadow of the steps. All eyes are turned towards the little child who is walking alone up the great stone staircase. On the topmost step the high priest advances to meet her, resplendent in his rich priestly garments.

The figure of the little Virgin is very quaint in a long gown made of some shimmering blue stuff. The golden hair is brushed back primly and woven into a heavy braid, whence it at last escapes in beautiful profusion. It would be hard to guess the child's age, for her demeanor is that of a little woman as she gathers her long skirt daintily in her right hand. She carries herself erect in the new dignity of the great moment, and advances with perfect self-confidence. The face, however, is quite childlike and innocent, and is lifted to the priest's with a happy smile. The left arm is raised in a gesture of wonder and delight.

The whole figure is surrounded by a halo of golden light. This is the oval-shaped glory which the Italians call the *mandorla,* from the word meaning "almond." It is of course the symbol of the virgin's peculiar sanctity. The painter has not tried to make the little girl particularly pretty, but he gives her the indescribable charm which we call winsomeness. She is perhaps one of the most lovable children art has ever produced.

As we study the artist's method of work in the picture we see how very simply the figure is drawn. Titian was fond of rich and voluminous draperies, as we shall learn from several examples which are to follow. Here, however, he draws a dress with tight sleeves and scanty skirt absolutely without decoration of any sort. It is this simplicity which gives the childlike appearance to the figure.

There is a pathos in the little figure which we cannot altogether appreciate in our illustration. We have to remember that the whole picture measures twenty-five feet in width by eleven in height, and then imagine how tiny the child looks ascending alone the great staircase in the centre of this vast panorama. The isolation of the figure suggests the singular destiny of Mary, set apart from others in the loneliness of a unique service.

III

THE EMPRESS ISABELLA

The most illustrious of Titian's many patrons was the Emperor Charles V., whose wife was the Empress Isabella of our portrait. This powerful monarch had inherited from one grandfather, Ferdinand, the kingdom of Spain, and from another, Maximilian, the empire of Germany. His marriage was arranged chiefly for political reasons, but proved to be a happy one.

Isabella was the daughter of Emmanuel the Great, late King of Portugal, and the sister of John III., the reigning king. She was a princess of uncommon beauty and accomplishments. The Portuguese government bestowed a superb dowry of nine hundred thousand crowns upon her, and the marriage was celebrated in Seville in 1526. The ceremony was splendid, and there were great festivities following.

Soon after, the emperor travelled with his bride through Andalusia and Granada that he might see his new kingdom. Called at last to other parts of his dominion, he left Isabella as regent in Spain, and went to Italy, where in 1532 he first called Titian into service to paint his portrait. In the years that followed the painter found the emperor a constant and generous patron, and was frequently summoned to meet the court at various places.

In the meantime, however, the lovely empress never had had a sitting to the first painter of the day. She stayed quietly at home and had her portrait painted by such inferior artists as were at hand.

When she died in 1539 Charles was left disconsolate, without any satisfactory portrait of her beloved face. He accordingly sent to Titian a portrait of her painted at the age of twenty-four, and required him to use it as the basis of a picture. The painter obeyed, and soon sent, his royal patron two canvases, begging him to return them with criticisms if he wished any changes made. As they were never sent back we infer that Charles found them as much like the original as could have been expected. The fame of Isabella's beauty and goodness had of course come to the painter's knowledge, and this was perhaps a better inspiration than the old portrait which was his guide. Certainly the picture he produced shows a winning personality.

The empress is seated near a window, holding a little book open in one hand, probably a prayer-book or Book of Hours. The lady is not reading, but gazes somewhat pensively before her, as if thinking over the familiar words. The face is gentle and refined, and has an innocent purity of expression like that of a child.

The features are small, and modelled with an almost doll-like regularity. Yet the mouth is set firmly enough to indicate a strong will behind it. Isabella was indeed a woman of remarkable self-control. A story is told that once when ill and in great pain she turned her face in the shadow that none might see her suffer, and uttered no sound of complaining. Her nurses remonstrated, but she replied firmly, "Die I may, but wail I will not."

The costume of a Spanish queen of the sixteenth century naturally interests us. Apparently Spanish Court etiquette of the period dictated a dress made with high neck and long sleeves. The bodice is of red velvet, the loose sleeves lined with satin. The under bodice, which we should call a *guimpe*, is of white muslin with gold fillets. A jewel adorns the red hair, and a long necklace of pearls is caught on the bosom with a pendant of rubies and emeralds. The careful dressing of the hair, the strict propriety of the gown, and the attitude of the queen herself suggest the regard of conventionality which governed the great lady.

What the portrait lacks is the quality of lifelikeness which makes other pictures by Titian so wonderful. [8] Naturally the painter could not so easily impart vitality to the picture when not working directly from the living model. To make up, as it were, for this defect, he painted the various textures of the dress with marvellous skill. Satin, velvet, and muslin, each is distinguished by its own peculiar lustre.

The bit of landscape seen through the window is another beautiful part of the picture. The distance gives depth to the composition and avoids the crowded effect it might otherwise have. We shall see a similar setting again in the portrait of Lavinia.

The Emperor had been very fond of his wife, and an old historian says that "he treated her on all occasions with much distinction and regard." If this seems nothing surprising to note, we must remember that at the same period Henry VIII. of England was treating his queens quite differently.

In the last years of his life Charles V., weary of the cares of government, relinquished his kingdom to his son. He retired to the convent of Yuste to end his days, taking with him this portrait of his wife. When he lay on his death-bed he asked to see the picture, and when at last he died his body was laid to rest beside Isabella. Their son, Philip II., whose portrait we are presently to study, succeeded to a portion of his father's dominion.

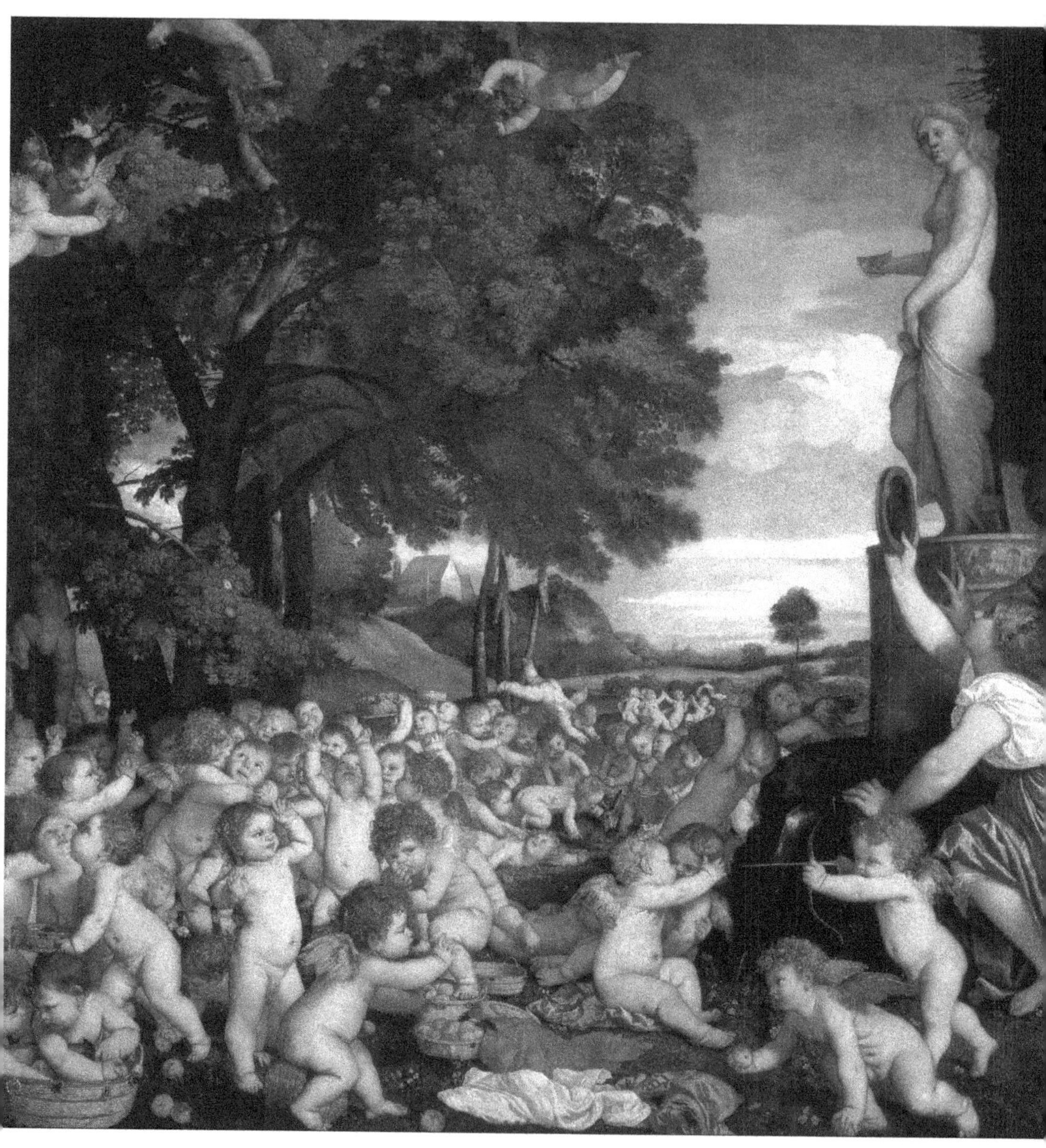

Titian, The Worship of Venus, 1518, Madrid

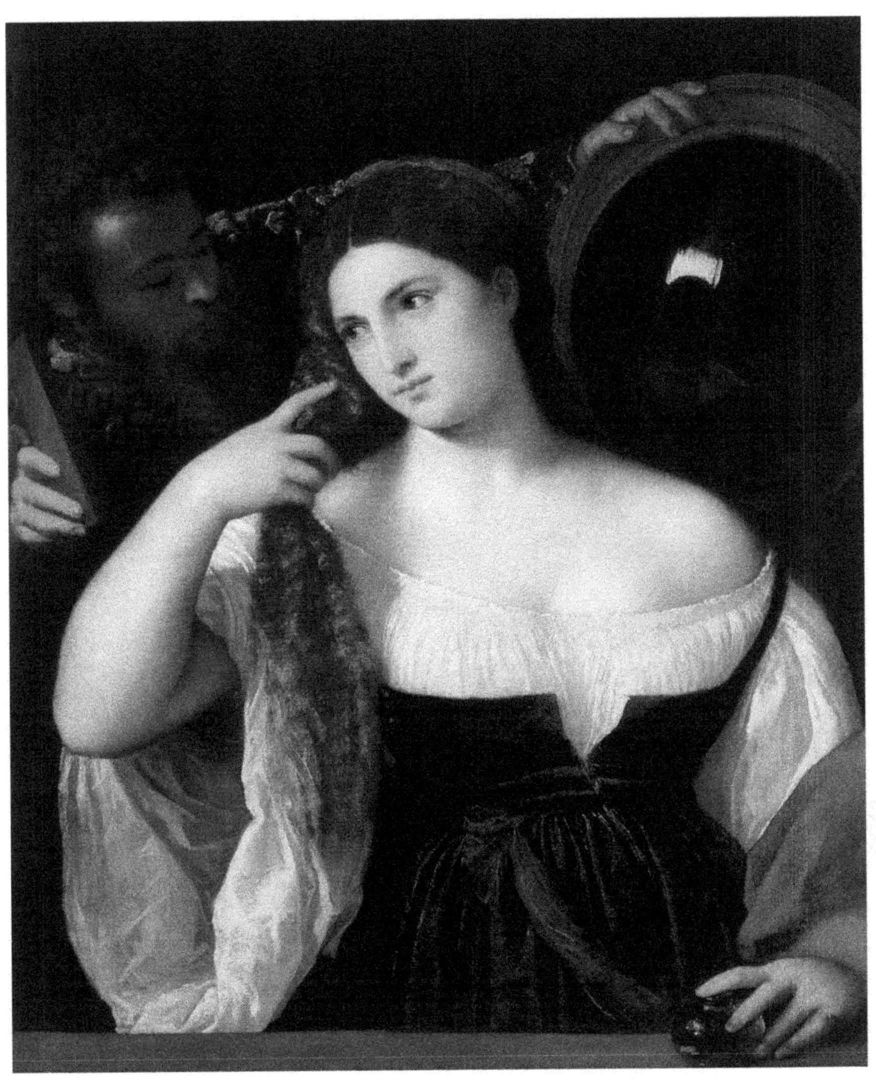

Titian, Woman With a Mirror, 1514, Louvre

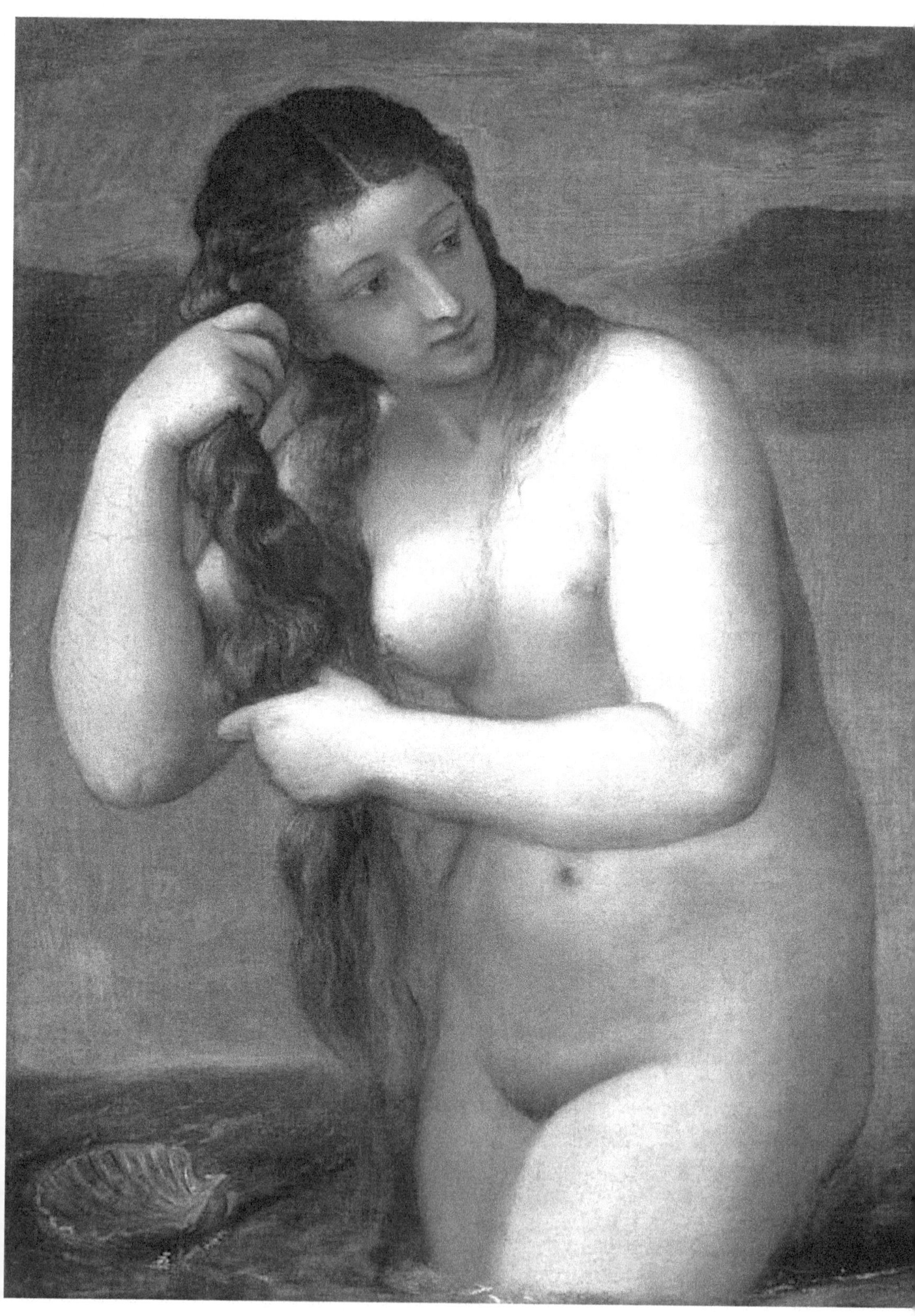

Titian, Venus Rising From the Sea, 1520, Scotland

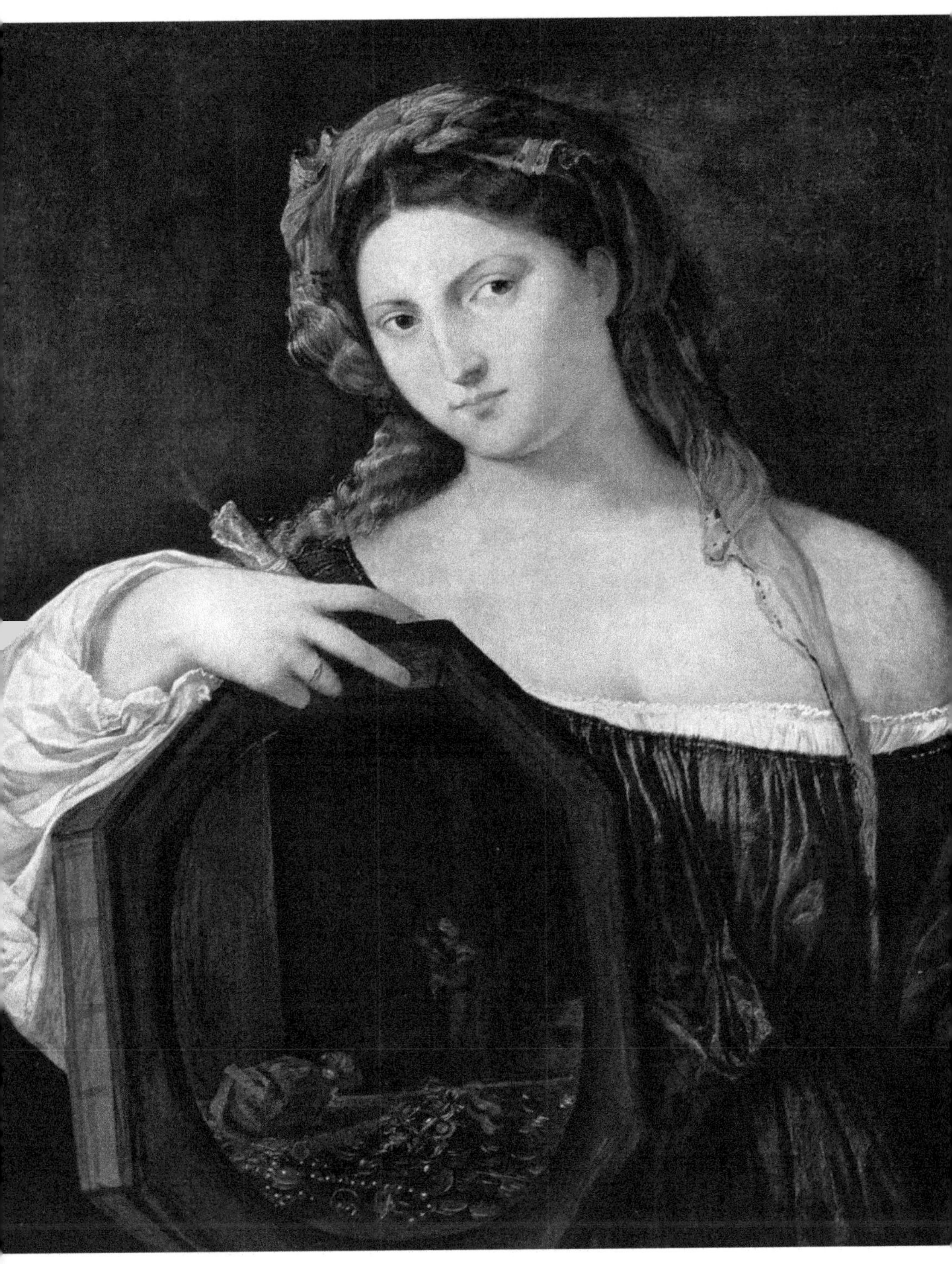

Titian, Vanita, 1511, Alte Pinakothek, München

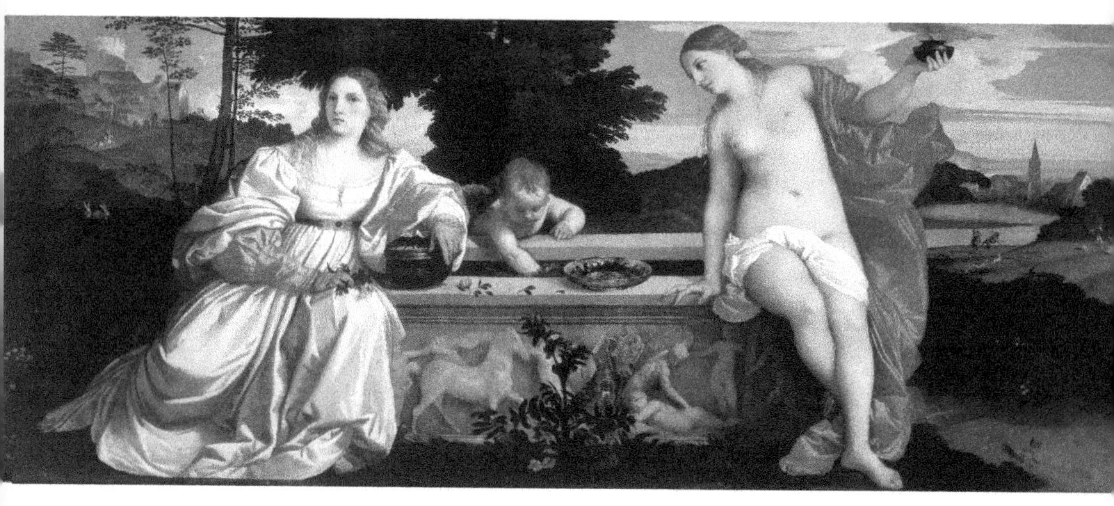

Titian, Sacred and Profane Love, 1514, Villa Borghese

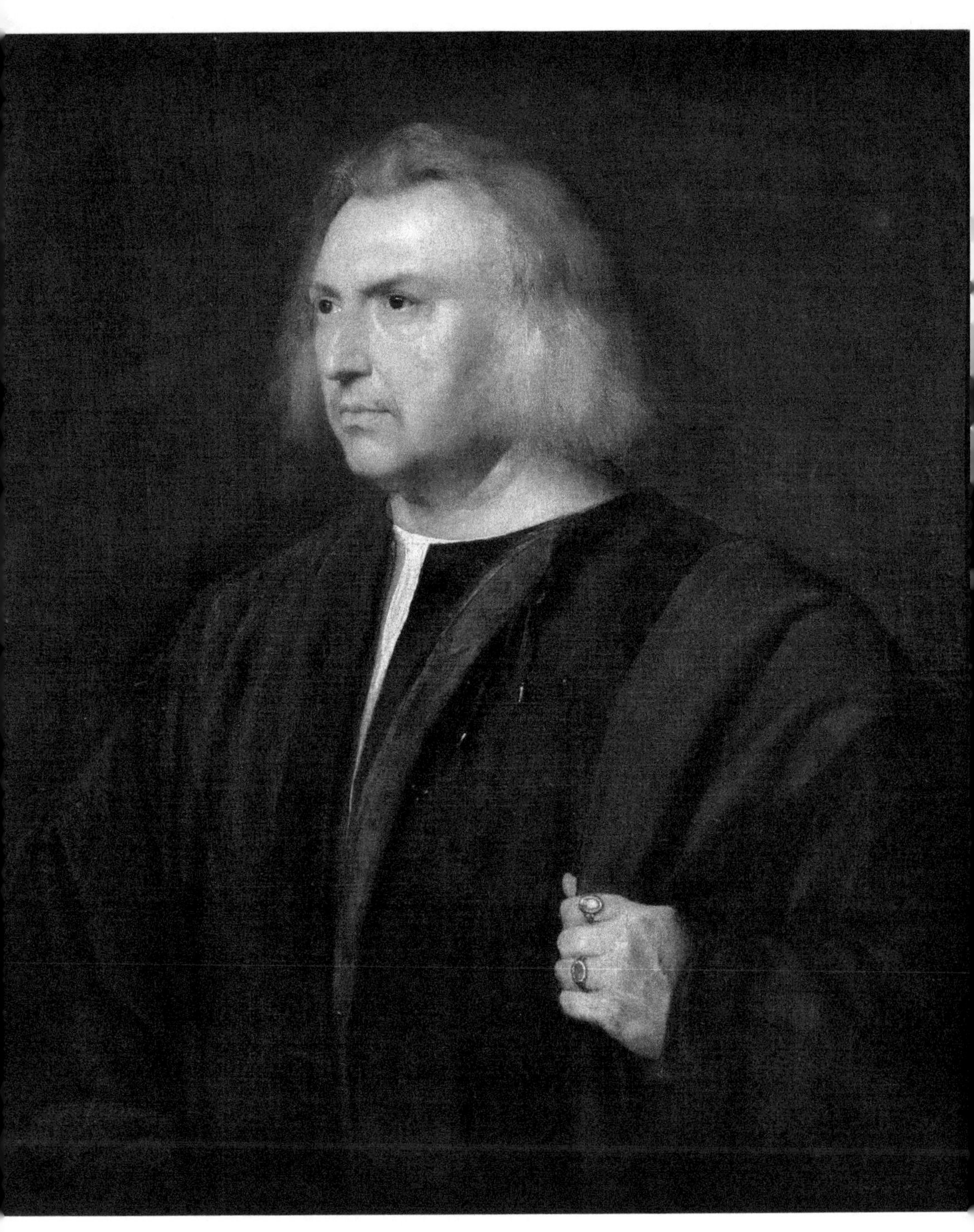

Titian, Gian Giacomo Bartolotti da Parma, 1518, Vienna

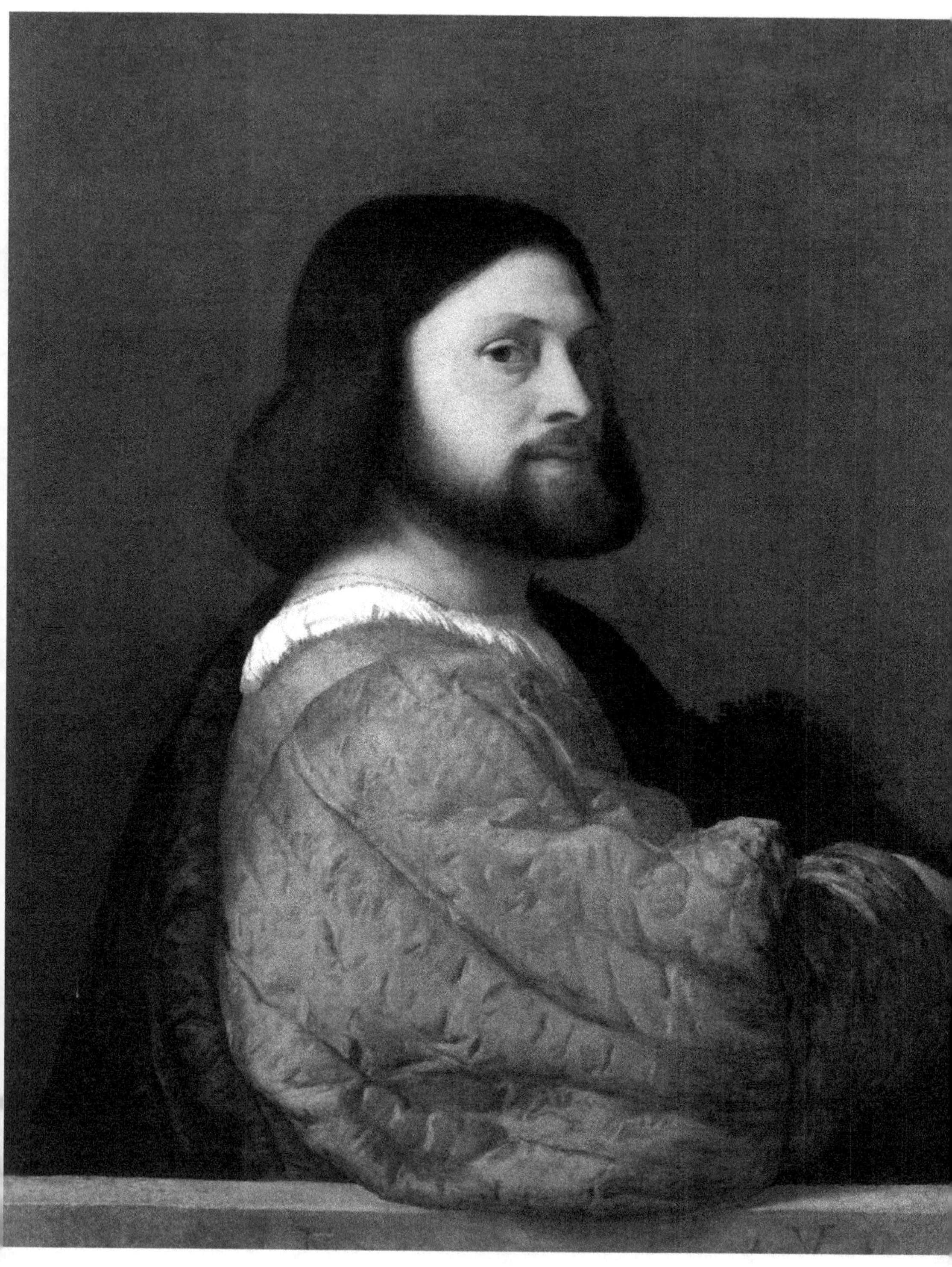

Titian, Man With the Blue Sleeve, 1510-11,
National Gallery, London

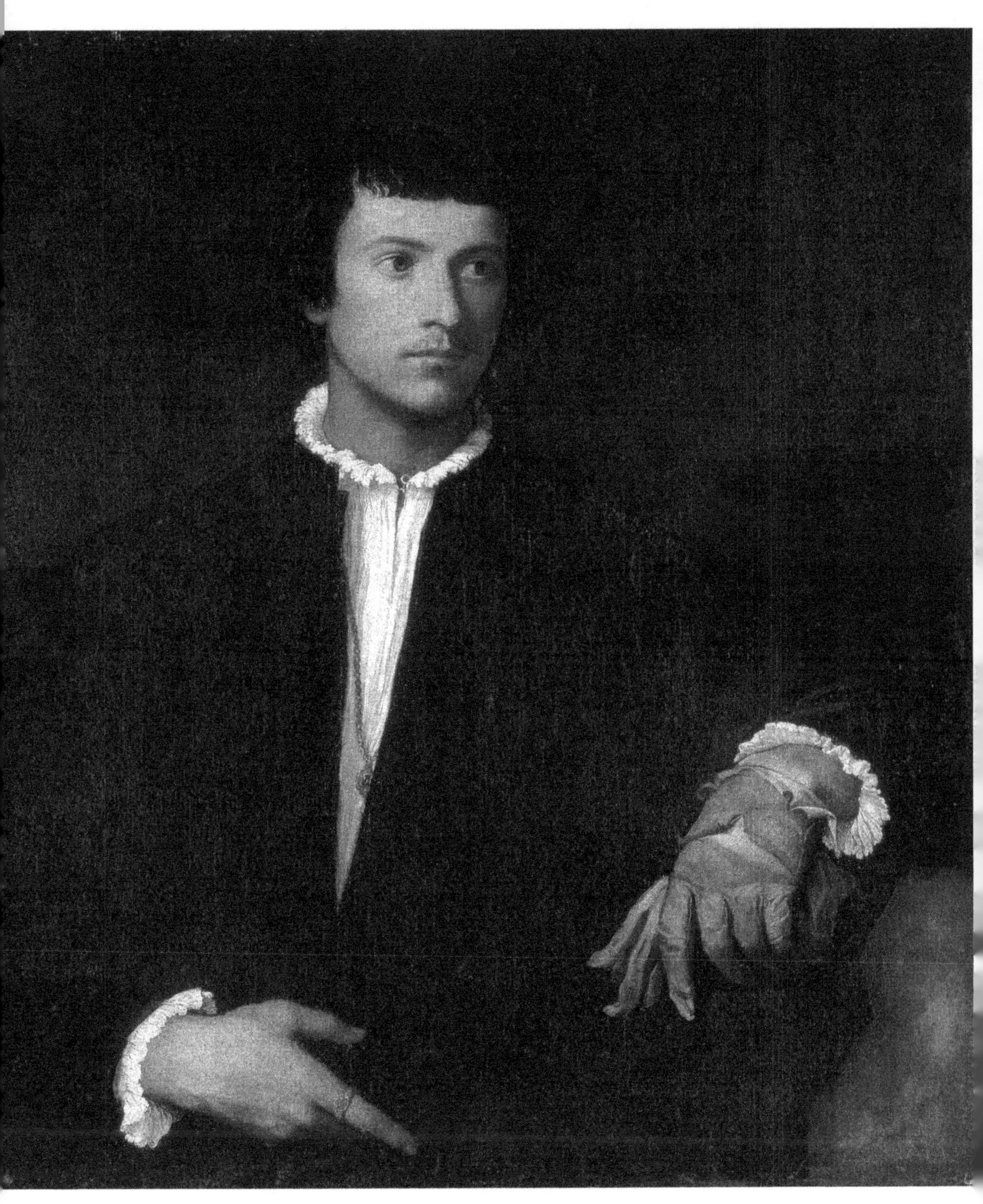

Titian, Man With a Glove, 1520, Louvre

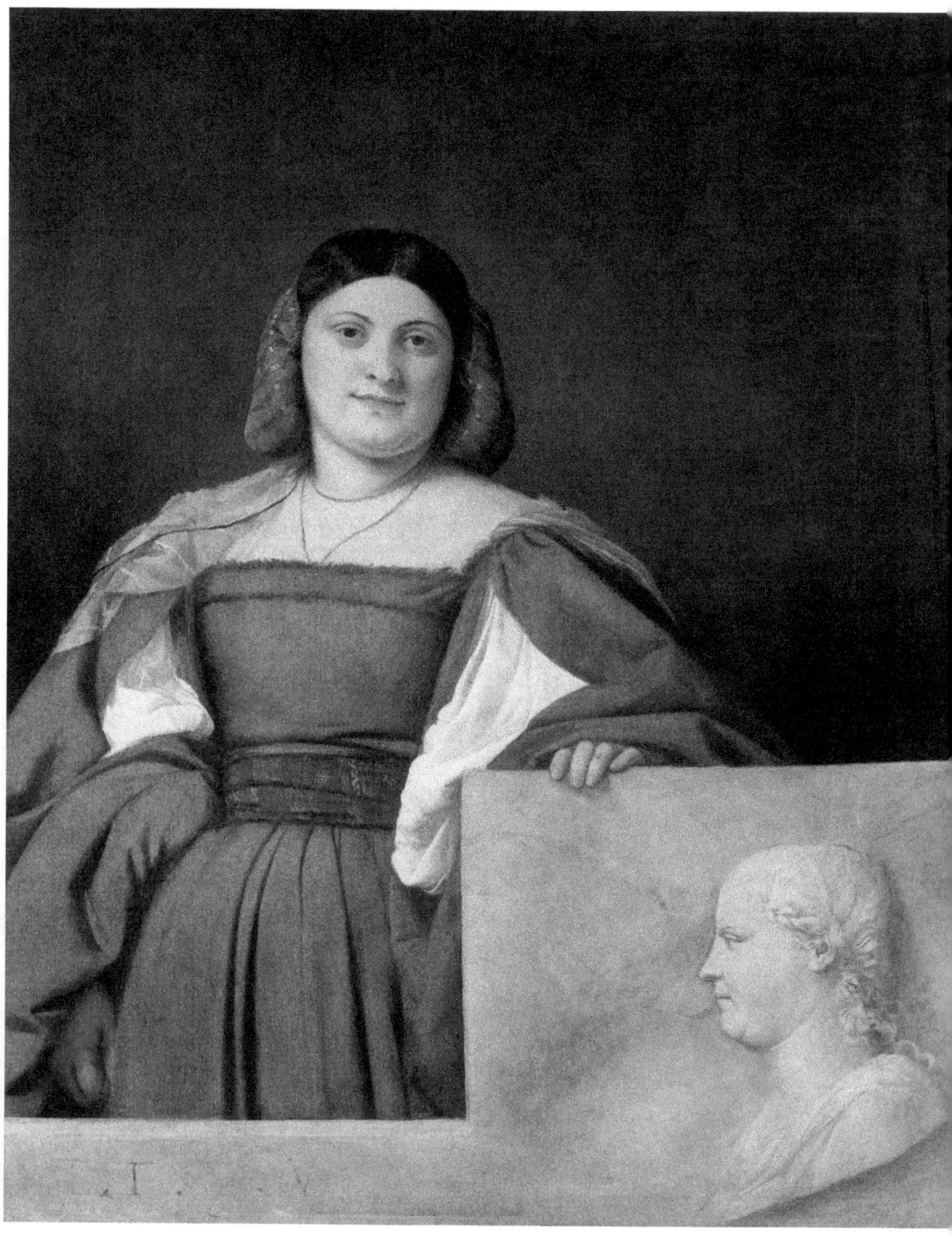

Titian, La Schiavona, 1510,
National Gallery, London

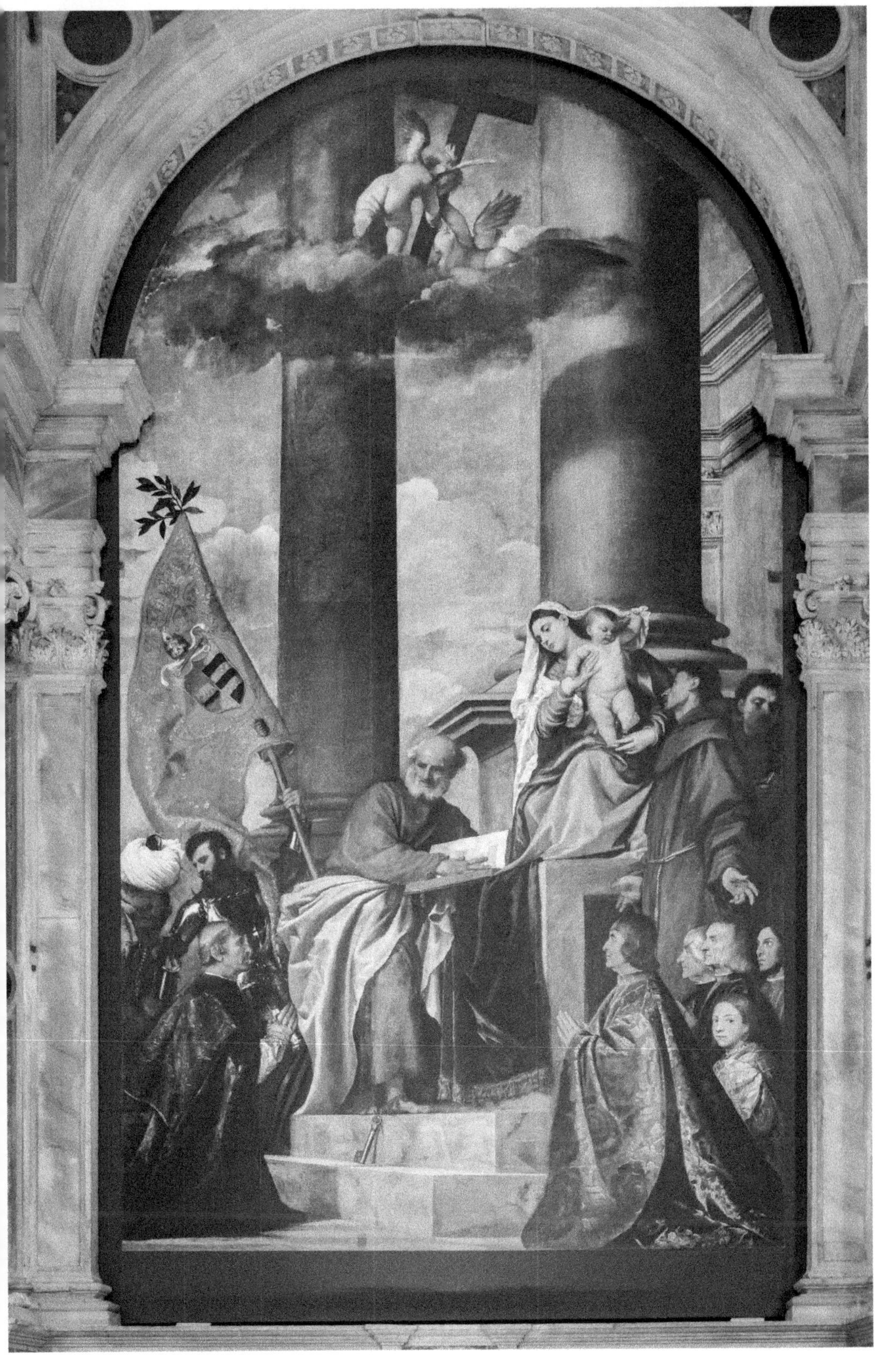

Titian, Pesaro Altarpiece, 1519-26, Friari , Venice

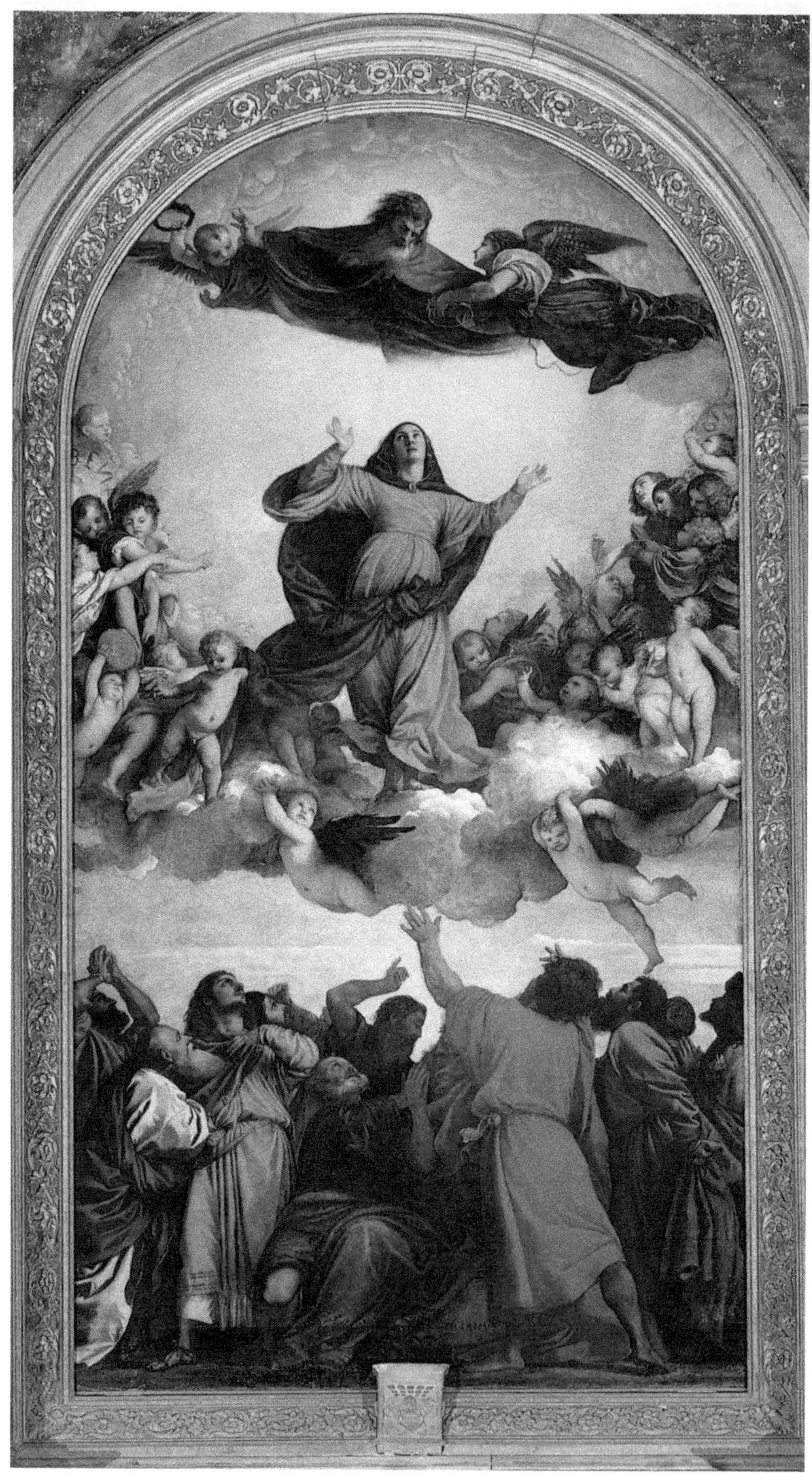

Titian, Assumption of the Virgin, 1517-18, Venice

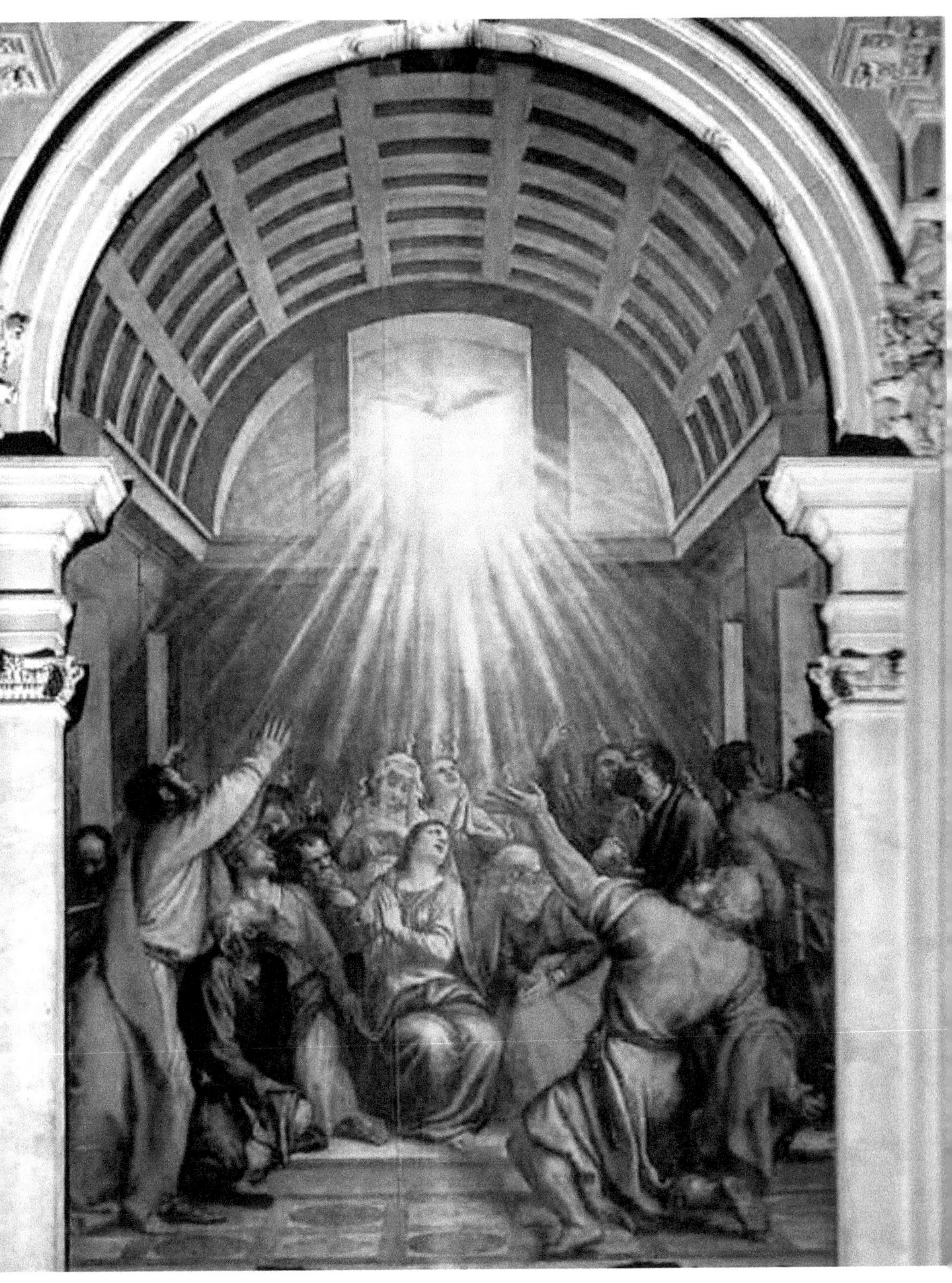

Titian, The Descent of the Holy Spirit, Venice

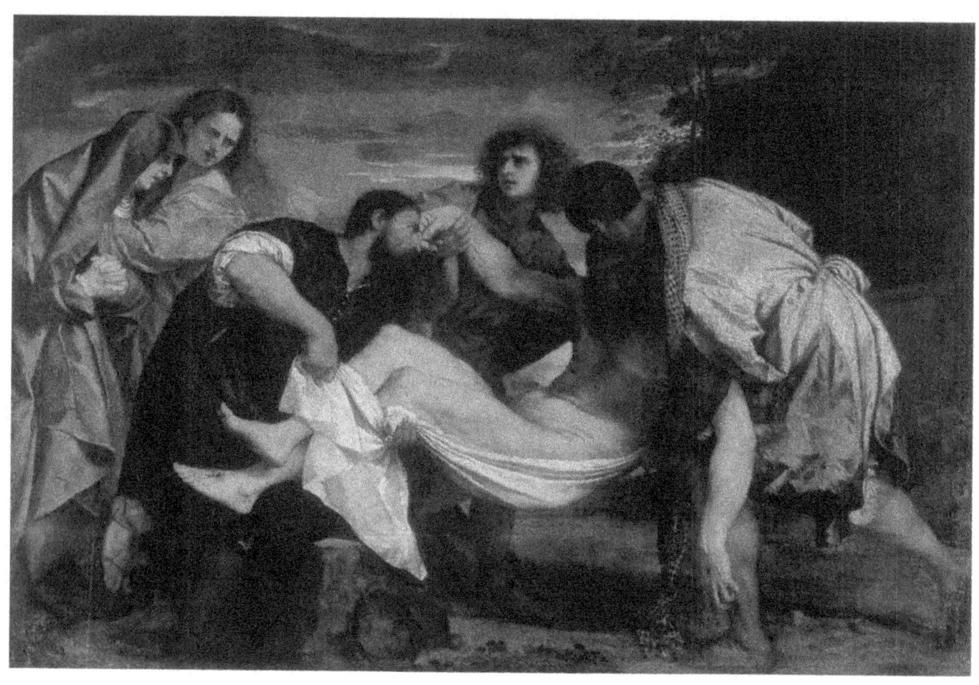

Titian, The Entombment, 1523-26, Louvre

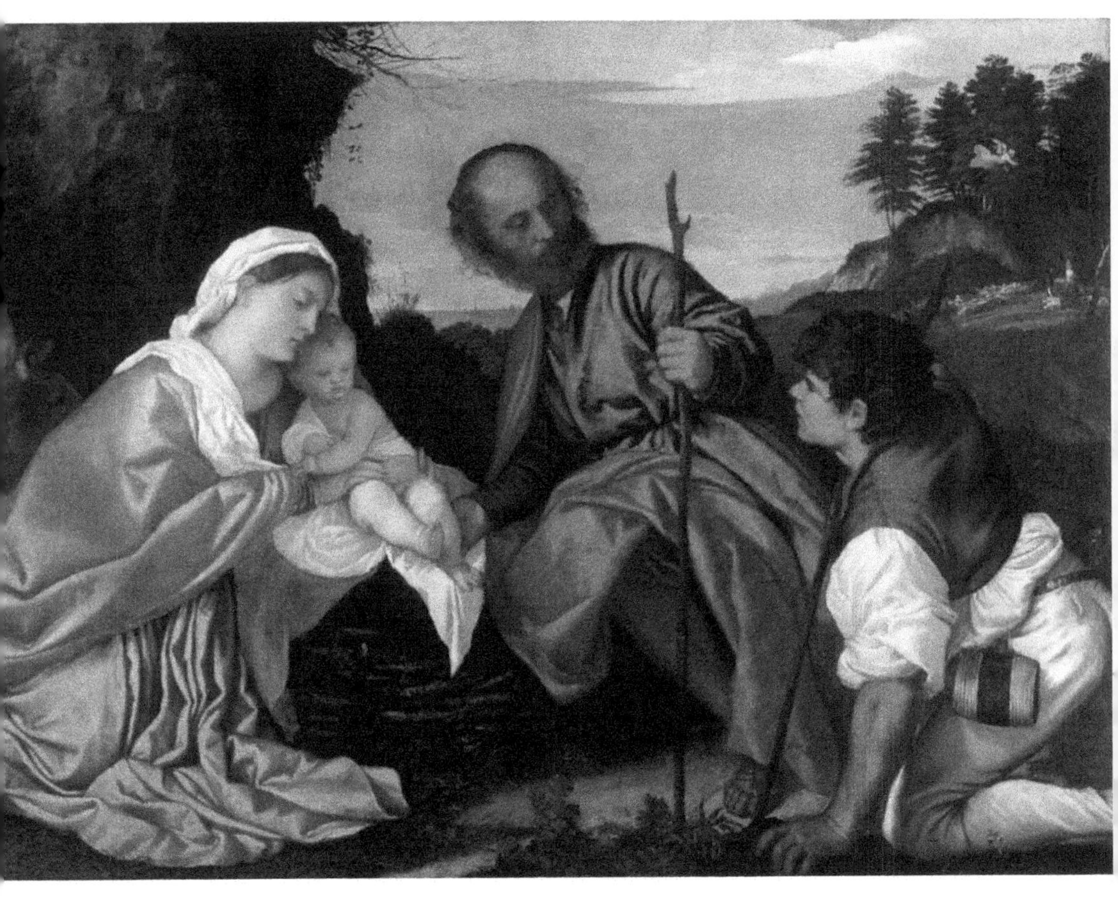

Titian, The Holy Family With a Shepherd, 1510,
National Gallery, Lndon

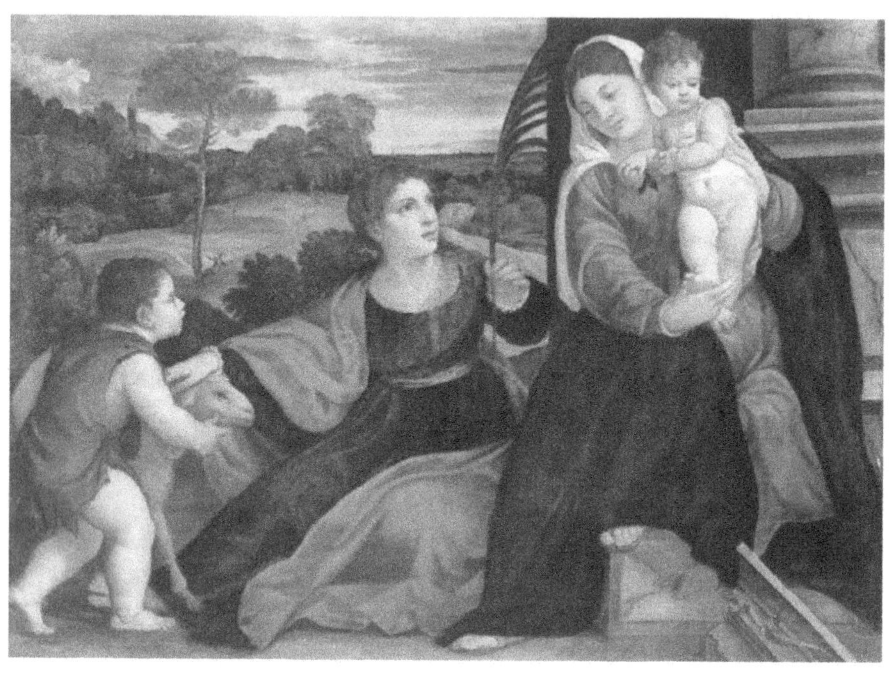

Titian, Madonna and Child With Saints Agnes and the Baptist, Dijon

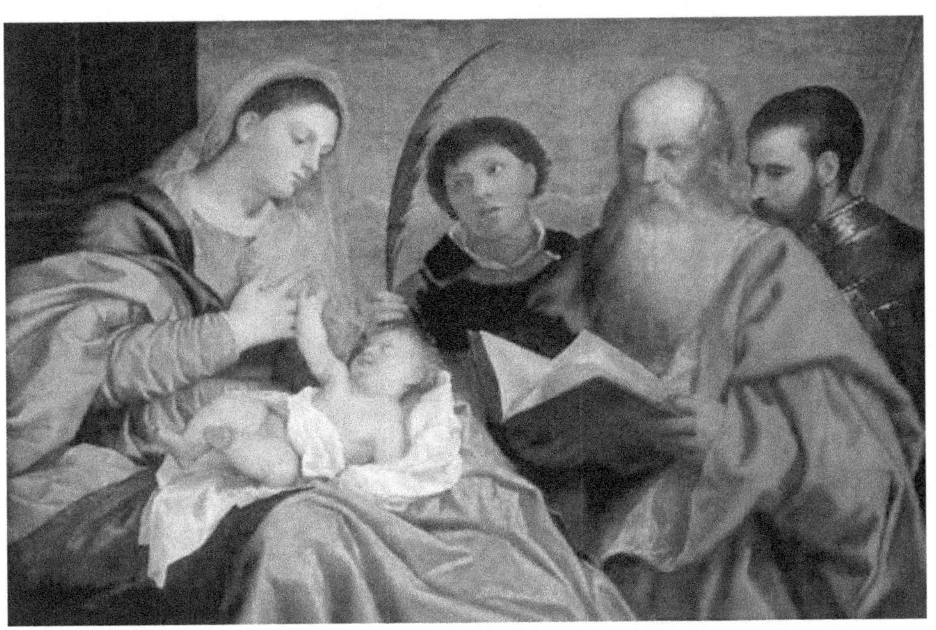

Titian, Madonna and Child With Saints, 1520, Vienna

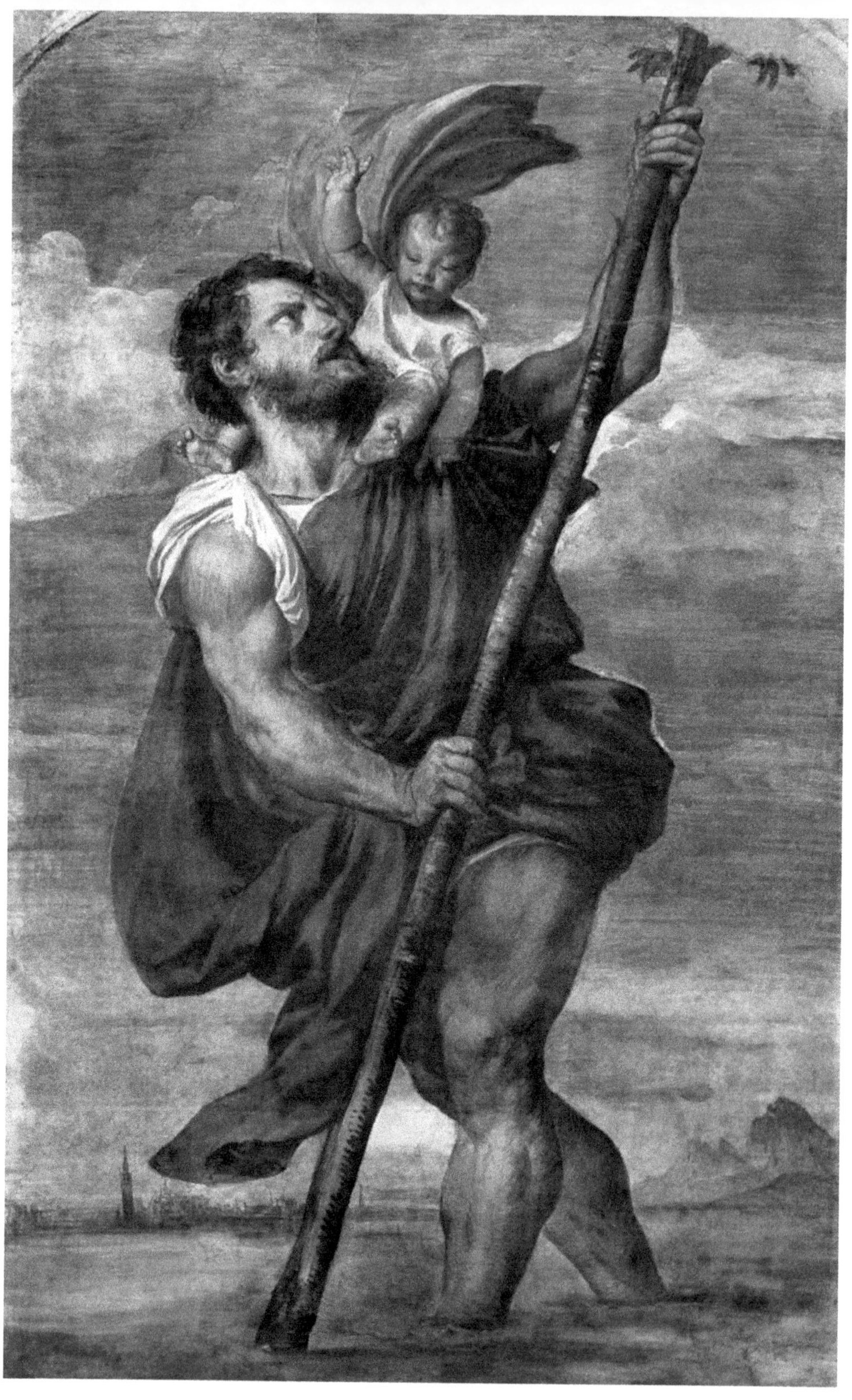

Titian, St Christopher, 1524, Venice

IV

MADONNA AND CHILD WITH SAINTS

There was never a child so longed for as the Child Jesus, and none whose infancy has been held in such loving remembrance. Centuries before his birth the prophets of Israel preached to the people of his coming. Year after year men waited eagerly for One who would teach them the way of righteousness. On the night when he was born the angels of heaven appeared in the sky with the glad tidings. His birthday ushered in a new era.

We all know the story of his infancy in the Bethlehem manger, of his boyhood in the little town of Nazareth, of the years of his ministry throughout Judea, and of his crucifixion on Calvary. The narrative of his life was written by the four evangelists, and has been told in nearly every part of the world.

Many of the great painters have drawn the subjects of their best pictures from the story in the Gospels. A favorite subject has been the mother Mary holding the Babe in her arms, as in our illustration. To understand why the other figures are included in the scene, a few words of explanation are necessary.

In the early days of Christianity the followers of the new faith had to endure great persecutions, and many laid down their lives for their Master. The religious liberty we enjoy to-day is due to the courage and loyalty of these early saints and martyrs. Much, too, is due to the work of those teachers who are called the Fathers of the church. These saints and heroes of the olden time have been honored in art and song and story. It is fitting to associate their memory with that of him to whom they gave their lives. This is the reason why in pictures of the Mother and Child Jesus we often see them standing by.

Such pictures do not represent any actual historical event. The various persons represented may not even be contemporaries. It is in a devotional and not a literal sense that they worship the Christ child together.

In our picture the Mother tends her Babe at one side while three saints form an attendant company. The nearest is St. Stephen, the young man "full of faith and power," who did "great wonders and miracles among the people" of Jerusalem in the apostolic days. When false witnesses accused him of blasphemy his face was like "the face of an angel." Nevertheless, when his accusers heard his defence they were angry at his frank denunciations, and casting him out of the city, stoned him to death. [9]

The old man standing next is St. Jerome, one of the Latin fathers of the fourth century. He was both a preacher and a writer, and his greatest service to the world was his translation of the Bible into Latin (the Vulgate). This is the book from which he is now reading, and St. George seems to look over his shoulder. St. George is the hero saint who rescued the princess Cleodolinda from the dragon. He suffered many tortures at the orders of the Emperor Diocletian, and was finally beheaded for his faith. [10]

We learn to identify these and other saints in the old pictures by certain features which the masters long ago agreed upon as appropriate to the characters. St. Stephen we recognize here because he is young, and carries a palm as the symbol of his martyrdom. St. Jerome is always an old man and is known here by his book, and St. George is distinguished by his armor.

The three make an interesting group as they represent three ages of man, - youth, maturity, and old age. They stand, too, for distinctly different temperaments. St. Stephen has the ardent imaginative nature of a dreamer, St. George the active prosaic temper of the warrior, and St. Jerome the grave contemplative mind of the scholar. Each serves the Christ with his own gift.

In the picture the three seem to be reading together some passage referring to the birth of Christ, perhaps that glorious verse from the prophet Isaiah, "Unto us a child is born, unto us a son is given." Coming to the words "Wonderful, Counsellor," St. Stephen lifts his face adoringly.

The Child is innocently unconscious of his grave guests. He lies across his mother's lap kicking his feet gleefully and looking up to her with a playful, appealing gesture. She bends over him smiling, and the two seem to talk together in the mystic language of babyhood. The artist, we see, painted the mother as beautiful and the child as winsome as he could well imagine them. He did not try to discover how a woman of Judea was likely to have looked centuries before. He preferred to think of Mary as one of the beautiful Venetian women of his own day. He may have seen some real mother and babe who suggested the picture to him, but in that case he painted them largely according to his own fancy. The Madonna's dress is not according to any Venetian fashions, but in the simple style chosen as most appropriate by old masters. Red and blue were the colors always used in her draperies, and it was also an ancient custom to represent her as wearing a veil over her head as befitting her modesty.

The mother has the fresh comely look of perfect health, yet with much delicacy and refinement in her gentle face. Both she and the babe seem to rejoice in abounding health and vitality. The picture is full of the joy of life.

V

PHILIP II

Philip II. was the son of the Emperor Charles V. and the Empress Isabella, whose portrait we have seen. He had therefore, like most princes, a union of several nationalities in his lineage. Upon his birth in 1527, all Spain rejoiced that there was now an heir to the throne. Charles himself counted eagerly upon the help his son would give him in the administration of his vast dominions.

From the first Philip was a grave and thoughtful child, pursuing his studies first with his mother and then with a tutor. When he was twelve years old his mother died; and two years later his father, who had scarcely seen the boy, returned to Spain, and devoted himself for a while to teaching him the principles of government. Philip was an apt pupil, and showed great fondness for statesmanship.

At the age of sixteen a great responsibility fell upon the young prince. Charles was called to Germany and left Philip as regent of Spain. A marriage had already been arranged between the youth and his cousin Mary of Portugal, and this took place soon after the Emperor's departure. Philip's regency was eminently successful, and he won the lasting affection and loyalty of the Spanish people.

The Emperor now planned that the prince should make a journey through the empire to become acquainted with his future subjects. The Spanish parted with him reluctantly, and he set forth accompanied by a great train of courtiers. Six months he was on his way, everywhere greeted by festivals, banquets and tourneys. Philip, being of a reticent and sombre nature, had little taste for these festivities, but having political ambition, submitted as gracefully as possible. At length he made a state entry into Brussels. This was in 1548; and in the two years that followed, the emperor and prince were together, planning their future policy of government. The lessons which Charles most deeply impressed upon Philip were those of self-repression, patience and distrust. The leading element in his policy was to be absolute ruler.

It was at the close of these two years, that is, in 1550, that the emperor, attending a diet in Augsburg, summoned thither Titian to paint the portrait of Philip. The prince was now in his twenty-fourth year, and stood, as it were, on the threshold of his great career. There could scarcely be a more unattractive subject for a portrait. Philip had a poor figure, with narrow chest and large ungainly feet, and his features were exceedingly ill-formed. His eyes were large and bulging, he had a projecting jaw and full fleshy lips which his scanty beard could not conceal. Titian, however, had the great artist's gift of making the most of a subject. We forget all Philip's defects when we look at this magnificent portrait.

The skill with which the splendid costume is painted would alone make the picture a great work of art. Philip wears a breastplate and hip pieces of armor, richly inlaid with gold, slashed embroidered hose, as the short trousers are called, white silk tights and white slippers. The collar of the Golden Fleece is the crowning ornament.

The attitude of the prince is full of dignity. He stands in front of a table on which his helmet and gauntlets are laid. The right hand rests on the helmet, and the left holds the hilt of the rapier which hangs at his side.

The most remarkable quality in the portrait is the impression of royalty it conveys. Though Philip has little to boast of in good looks, he has inherited from generations of royal ancestors that indefinable air of distinction which belongs to his station. It is this which the painter has expressed in his attitude and bearing.

Young as the face is, with little of life's experience to give it individuality, the painter makes it a revelation of the leading elements in Philip's character. The seriousness of the boy has developed into the habitual gravity of the man. Already we see how well the father's lessons have been learned, how self-contained and cautious the prince has become. The affairs of state seem to weigh heavily upon him.

The proportions of the figure to the size and shape of the canvas add something to the apparent height of Philip. Titian has done everything a painter could do to give an ill-favored prince an appearance befitting his royal prestige: it is a kingly portrait.

Three years after it was painted, the picture was sent to England to be shown to Queen Mary. Philip, now a widower, had become a suitor of the English queen. The report came that Mary was "greatly enamoured" of the portrait, and the marriage was soon after effected. Philip, however, did not win great favor with the English, and after Mary's death he chose a French princess for his next wife, and spent his life in Spain.

Upon the abdication of his father, he became the most powerful monarch in Europe, and had the best armies of his time. He was constantly at war with other nations, usually two or more at a time, and by undertaking too many schemes often failed. It was during his reign that the Netherlands were lost to Spain, and the famous Spanish Armada was destroyed by the English.

VI

SAINT CHRISTOPHER

There was once in the land of Canaan a giant named Offero, which means "the bearer." His colossal size and tremendous strength made him an object of terror to all beholders, and he determined to serve none but the most powerful being in the world.

He accordingly joined the retinue of a great king, and for a while all went well. One day while listening to a minstrel's song, the king trembled and crossed himself every time the singer mentioned the Devil. "Then," thought Offero, "there is one more powerful than the King; and he it is whom I should serve." So he went in search of the Devil, and soon entered the ranks of his army.

One day as they came to a wayside cross he noticed his master tremble and turn aside. "Then," thought Offero, "there is one more powerful than the Devil, and he it is whom I should serve." He now learned that this greater being whom the Devil feared was Jesus, who died on the cross, and he earnestly sought to know the new Master.

An old hermit undertook to instruct him in the faith. "You must fast," said he. "That I will not," said Offero, "lest I lose my strength." "You must pray," said the hermit. "That I cannot," said Offero. "Then," said the hermit, "go to the river side and save those who perish in the stream." "That I will," said Offero joyfully.

The giant built him a hut on the bank and rooted up a palm tree from the forest to use as a staff. Day and night he guided strangers across the ford and carried the weak on his shoulders. He never wearied of his labor.

One night as he rested in his hut he heard a child's voice calling to him from the shore, "Offero, come forth, and carry me over." He arose and went out, but seeing nothing returned and lay down. Again the voice called, "Offero, come forth and carry me over." Again he went out and saw no one. A third time the voice came, "Offero, come forth, and carry me over."

The giant now took a lantern, and by its light found a little child sitting on the bank, repeating the cry, "Offero, carry me over." Offero lifted the child to his great shoulders, and taking his staff strode into the river. The wind blew, the waves roared, and the water rose higher and higher, yet the giant pushed bravely on. The burden which had at first seemed so light grew heavier and heavier. Offero's strong knees bent under him, and it seemed as if he would sink beneath the load. Yet on he pressed with tottering steps, never complaining, until at last the farther bank was reached. Here he set his precious burden gently down, and looking with wonder at the child, asked, "Who art thou, child? The burden of the world had not been heavier." "Wonder not," said the Child, "for thou hast borne on thy shoulders him who made the world." Then a bright light shone about the little face, and in another moment the mysterious stranger had vanished. Thus was it made known to Offero that he had been taken into the service of the most powerful being in the world. From this time forth he was known as Christ-offero, or Christopher, the Christ-bearer. [11]

With this story in mind we readily see the meaning of our picture. The giant has reached mid-stream, with his tiny passenger perched astride his shoulders. Already the burden has become mysteriously heavy, and Offero bends forward to support the strain, staying himself with his great staff. He lifts his face to the child's with an expression of mingled anguish and wonder.

The situation is full of strange pathos. The babe seems so small and helpless beside the splendid muscular strength of the brawny giant. Yet he is here the leader. With uplifted hand he seems to be cheering his bearer on the toilsome way.

The figures in the picture seem to be taken from common every-day life. Some Venetian boatman may have been the painter's model for St. Christopher, whose attitude is similar to that of a gondolier plying his oar. The child, too, is a child of the people, a sturdy little fellow, quite at ease in his perilous position. We shall understand better the range of Titian's art by contrasting these more commonplace figures with the refined and elegant types we see in some of our other illustrations.

The picture of St. Christopher is a fresco painting on the walls of the palace of the doges or dukes in Venice. It was originally designed to celebrate the arrival of the French army in 1523, at an Italian town called San Cristoforo. It is so placed that it might be the first object seen every morning when the doge left his bed-chamber. This was on account of an old tradition that the sight of St. Christopher always gives courage to the beholder. "Whoever shall behold the image of St. Christopher, on that day shall not faint or fail," runs an old Latin inscription.

As fresco painting was a method of art comparatively unfamiliar to Titian, it is interesting to know than an eminent critic pronounces our picture "broad and solid in execution, rich and brilliant in color." [12] We see from our reproduction that the paint has flaked from the wall in a few places.

VII

LAVINIA

Something of the home life of Titian must be known in order to understand the loving care which he bestowed upon this portrait of his daughter Lavinia. The painter's works were in such demand that he could afford to live in a costly manner. He had a true Venetian's love of luxury, and liked to surround himself with elegant things. His society was sought by rich noblemen, and he himself lived like a prince.

When somewhat over fifty years of age Titian removed to a spot just outside Venice in the district of Biri, where he laid out a beautiful garden. The view from Casa Grande, as the house was called, was very extensive, looking across the lagoon to the island of Murano and the hills of Ceneda. Here Titian entertained his guests with lavish hospitality. A distinguished scholar of that time, one Priscianese, who had come to Venice in 1540 to publish a grammar, describes how he was entertained there: "Before the tables were set out," he writes, ... "we spent the time in looking at the lively figures in the excellent pictures, of which the house was full, and in discussing the real beauty and charm of the garden.... In the meanwhile came the hour for supper, which was no less beautiful and well arranged than copious and well provided.

Besides the most delicate viands and precious wines, there were all those pleasures and amusements that are suited to the season, the guests and the feast.... The sea, as soon as the sun went down, swarmed with gondolas, adorned with beautiful women, and resounded with the varied harmony of music of voices and instruments, which till midnight accompanied our delightful supper."

The darling of this beautiful home at Casa Grande was the painter's daughter Lavinia, and the portrait shows how she looked in 1549. Her mother had died before the removal of the family to Biri, and the aunt, who had since tried to fill the vacant place, died about the time this portrait was painted. A new responsibility had therefore fallen upon the young girl, and she was now her father's chief consolation. It is thought that the picture was painted for Titian's friend Argentina Pallavicino of Reggio. As a guest at her father's house this gentleman must often have seen and admired the charming girl, and the portrait was a pleasant souvenir of his visits.

Lavinia is seen carrying a silver salver of fruit, turning, as she goes, to look over her shoulder. The open country stretches before her, and it is as if she were stepping from a portico of the house to the garden terrace to bring the fruit to some guest. She is handsomely dressed, as her father would like to see his daughter. The gown is of yellow flowered brocade, the bodice edged with jewelled cording. Over the neck is thrown a delicate scarf of some gauzy stuff, the ends floating down in front. An ornamental gold tiara is set on the wavy auburn hair, an ear-ring hangs from the pretty ear, and a string of pearls encircles the neck. Imagine the figure against a deep red curtain, and you have in mind the whole color scheme of this richly decorative picture.

Lavinia, however, would be attractive in any dress, with her fresh young beauty and simple unconscious grace. Her features are not modelled in classic lines: the charm of the face is its fresh color, the pretty curves of the plump cheek, and, above all, the sweet open expression. The hands are delicate and shapely, as of one well born and gently reared. Lavinia is perhaps not a very intellectual person, but she has a sweet sunny nature and is full of life and spirits. It would seem impossible to be sad or lonely in her cheery company. She holds her precious burden high, with an air of triumph, and turns with a smile to see it duly admired. The delicious fruit certainly makes a tempting display. The girl's innocent round face and arch pose remind one of a playful kitten.

The painter has chosen a graceful and unusual attitude. The curves of the outstretched arms serve as counterbalancing lines to the main lines of the figure. The artist himself was so pleased with the pose that he repeated it in another picture, where Lavinia assumes the gruesome rôle of Salome, and carries in her salver, in place of the fruit, the head of St. John the Baptist!

A few years after our portrait was painted, Lavinia was betrothed to Cornelio Sarcinelli, of Serravalle, and a new portrait was painted in honor of the event. When the marriage settlement was signed Lavinia brought her husband a dowry of fourteen hundred ducats, a royal sum in those days. The wedding was on the 19th of June, 1555.

Some years after her marriage Lavinia again sat to her father for her portrait. Her beauty, as we have noted, was not of a lasting kind, and in the passing years her fresh color faded, and she became far too stout for grace. Yet the frank nature always made her attractive, and it is pleasant to see in the kindly face the fulfilment of the happy promise of her girlhood.

VIII

CHRIST OF THE TRIBUTE MONEY

During the three years of Christ's ministry, his words and actions were closely watched by his enemies, who hoped to find some fault of which they could accuse him. Not a flaw could be seen in that blameless life, and it was only by some trick that they could get him into their power.

One plan that they devised was very cunning. Palestine was at that time a province of the Roman empire, and the popular party among the Jews chafed at having to pay tribute to the emperor Cæsar. On the other hand the presence of the Roman governor in Jerusalem made it dangerous to express any open rebellion. Jesus was the friend of the people, and many of his followers believed that he would eventually lead them to throw off the Roman yoke. As a matter of fact, however, he had taken no part in political discussions.

His enemies now determined to make him commit himself to one party or the other. If he declared himself for Rome, his popularity was lost; if against Rome he was liable to arrest. The evangelists relate how shrewdly their question was framed to force a compromising reply, and how completely he silenced them with his twofold answer. This is the story:-

> "Then went the Pharisees, and took counsel how they might entangle him in his talk. And they sent out unto him their disciples with the Herodians, saying, Master, we know that thou art true, and teachest the way of God in truth, neither carest thou for any man: for thou regardest not the person of men. Tell us therefore, What thinkest thou? Is it lawful to give tribute unto Cæsar, or not?
>
> "But Jesus perceived their wickedness, and said, Why tempt ye me, ye hypocrites? Shew me the tribute money. And they brought unto him a penny. And he saith unto them, Whose is this image and superscription? They say unto him, Cæsar's. Then saith he unto them, Render, therefore, unto Cæsar the things which are Cæsar's; and unto God the things that are God's. When they had heard these words, they marvelled and left him, and went their way."[13]

That was indeed a wonderful scene, and it is made quite real to us in our picture: Christ and the Pharisee stand face to face, engaged in conversation. A wily old fellow has been chosen spokesman for his party. His bronzed skin and hairy muscular arm show him to be of a common class of laborers. The face is seamed with toil, and he has the hooked, aquiline nose of his race. As he peers into the face of his supposed dupe, his expression is full of low cunning and hypocrisy. He holds between thumb and forefinger the Roman coin which Christ has called for, and looks up as if wondering what that has to do with the question.

Christ turns upon him a searching glance which seems to read his motives as an open page. There is no indignation in the expression, only sorrowful rebuke. His answer is ready, and he points quietly to the coin with the words which so astonish his listeners.

The character of Christ is so many-sided that any painter who tries to represent him has the difficult task of uniting in a single face all noble qualities of manhood. Let us notice what elements of character Titian has made most prominent, and we shall see how much more nearly he satisfies our ideal than other painters.

Refinement and intellectual power impress us first in this

countenance: the noble forehead is that of a thinker. The eyes show penetration and insight: we feel how impossible it would be to deceive this man. It is a gentle face, too, but without weakness. Here is one who would sympathize with the sorrowing and have compassion on the erring, but who would not forget to be just. Strength of character and firmness of purpose are indicated in his expression. The highest quality in the face is its moral earnestness. Its calm purity contrasts with the coarse, evil face of the questioner as light shining in the darkness. There is, perhaps, only one other head of Christ in art with which it can properly be compared, and this is by Leonardo da Vinci, in the Last Supper at Milan. The two painters have expressed, as no others have been able to, a spiritual majesty worthy of the subject.

The early painters used to surround the head of Christ with a circle of gold, which was called a nimbus, a halo, or a glory. The custom had been given up by Titian's time, but we see in our picture the remnant of the old symbol in the three tiny points of light which shine over the top and sides of the Saviour's hair. They are a mystic emblem of the Trinity.

The artistic qualities of the picture are above praise. There are few, if any, of Titian's works executed with so much care and delicacy of finish, but without sacrificing anything in the breadth. We recognize the painter's characteristic touch in the disposition of the draperies, in the delicacy of the hair, the modelling of the hands, and the pose of Christ's head. The figures have that quality of vitality which we observe in Titian's great portraits. The color of Christ's robe is red, and his mantle a deep blue.

IX

THE BELLA

Among Titian's wealthy patrons was a certain Duke of Urbino, Francesco Maria della Rovere, who, as the general-in-chief of the Venetian forces, came to Venice to live when our artist was at the height of his fame. From this time till the Duke's death the painter was brought into relations with this noble family. This was the period when the Bella was painted, and the picture has, as we shall see, an intimate connection with these patrons.

The Duke's wife was Eleanora Gonzaga, sister of the Duke of Mantua, celebrated for her beauty and refinement. A contemporary (Baldassare Castiglione) writing of the lady, says: "If ever there were united wisdom, grace, beauty, genius, courtesy, gentleness, and refined manners, it was in her person, where these combined qualities form a chain adorning her every movement."

The Duke himself was deeply in love with his wife. A week after his marriage he wrote that "he had never met a more comely, merry, or sweet girl, who to a most amiable disposition added a surprisingly precocious judgment, which gained for her general admiration." Eleanora, on her part A showed an undeviating affection for her husband, and they lived together happily.

From the date of her marriage, we can reckon that the Duchess must have been well into her thirties when she came to Venice to live. From a portrait Titian painted of her, when she was about forty, we see that much of the fresh beauty of her girlhood had faded. She had, however, good features, with large, fine eyes and arching brows. Her figure was graceful and her neck beautiful: the head was particularly well set.

All these qualities kindled the artistic imagination of Titian. In the matron of forty his inner eye caught a vision of the belle of twenty. Thereupon, he wrought an artist's miracle: he painted pictures of Eleanora as she had looked twenty years before. One of these, and perhaps the most famous, is the Bella of our illustration.[14] The identity of the original is hidden under this simple title, which is an Italian word, meaning the Beauty. An ancient legend tells of a wonderful fountain, by drinking of which a man, though old, might renew his youth and be, like the gods, immortal. There were some who went in quest of these waters, among them, as we remember, the Spanish knight, Ponce de Leon, who, thinking to find them north of Cuba, discovered our Florida. The Duchess of Urbino found such a fountain of youth in the art of Titian. Comparing her actual portrait with the Bella, painted within a few years, it seems as if the lady of the former had quaffed the magic draught which had restored her to her youthful beauty.

The Bella is what is called a half length portrait, the figure standing, tall, slender, and perfectly proportioned. The lady turns her face to meet ours, and whether we move to the right or the left, the eyes of the enchantress seem to follow us. We fall under their spell at the first glance; there is a delightful witchery about them.

The small head is exquisitely modelled, and the hair is coiled about it in close braids to preserve the round contours corresponding to the faultless curves of cheek and chin. The hair is of golden auburn, waving prettily about the face, and escaping here and there in little tendrils. Over the forehead it forms the same perfect arch which is repeated in the brows. The slender throat is long and round, like the stalk of a flower; the neck and shoulders are white and firm, and shaped in beautiful curves.

The rich costume interests us as indicating the fashions in the best Venetian society of the early 16th century. Comparing it with that of the Empress Isabella in our other picture, we notice that at the same period the Venetian styles differed considerably from the Spanish, to the advantage of the former. Instead of the stiff Spanish corset which destroyed the natural grace of the figure, the Bella wears a comfortably fitting bodice, from which the skirt falls in full straight folds. The dress is of brownish purple velvet, combined with peacock blue brocade. The sleeves are ornamented with small knots pulled through slashes. A long chain falls across the neck, and jewelled ear-rings hang in the ears.[15]

It is pleasant to analyze the details of the figure and costume, but after all the charm of the picture is in the total impression it conveys. Applied to this lovely vision of womanhood the words of Castiglione seem no flattery. In her are united "grace, beauty, courtesy, gentleness, and refined manners." The essence of aristocracy is expressed in her bearing: the pose of the head is that of a princess. There is no trace of haughtiness in her manner, and no approach to familiarity: she has the perfect equipoise of good breeding.

The picture gives us that sense of a real presence which it was the crowning glory of Titian's art to achieve. The canvas is much injured, but the Bella is still immortally young and beautiful.

X

MEDEA AND VENUS

(Formerly called Sacred and Profane Love)

A charming story is told in Ovid's "Metamorphoses" of Jason's adventures in search of the golden fleece, and of his love for Medea.[16] Jason was a Greek prince, young, handsome, brave, and withal of noble heart. He had journeyed over seas in his good ship Argo, and had at last come to Colchis to win the coveted treasure.

The King Æëtes had no mind to give up the fleece without a struggle, and he set the young hero a hard task. He was ordered to tame two bulls which had feet of brass and breath of flame. When he had yoked these, he was to plough a field and sow it with serpent's teeth which would yield a crop of armed men to attack him. While Jason turned over in his mind how he should perform these feats, he chanced to meet the king's beautiful daughter Medea. At once the two fell in love with each other, and Jason's fortunes took a new turn. Medea possessed certain secrets of enchantment which might be of practical service to her lover in his adventure. She had a magic salve which protected the body from fire and steel. She also knew the charm – and it was merely the throwing of a stone – which would turn the "earth-born crop of foes" from attacking an enemy to attack one another. Finally she had drugs which would put to sleep the dragon guarding the fleece.

To impart these secrets to Jason might seem an easy matter, but Medea did not find it so. She was a loyal daughter, and Jason had come to take her father's prized possession. She would be a traitor to aid a stranger against her own people. The poet tells how in her trouble the princess sought a quiet spot where she might take counsel with herself.

> "In vain," she cried,
> "Medea! dost thou strive! Some deity
> Resists thee! Ah, this passion sure, or one
> Resembling this, must be what men call love!
> Why should my sire's conditions seem too hard?
> And yet too hard they are! Why should I shake
> And tremble for the fate of one whom scarce
> These eyes have looked on twice? Whence comes this fear
> I cannot quell? Unhappy! from thy breast
> Dash out these new-lit fires! - Ah! wiser far
> If so I could! - But some new power constrains,
> And reason this way points, and that way, love."

The struggle goes on for some time, and the maiden's heart is torn with conflicting impulses. Summoning up "all images of right and faith and shame and natural duty," she fancies that her love is conquered. A moment later Jason crosses her path and the day is lost. Together they pledge their vows at the shrine of Hecate, and in due time they sail away in the Argo with the golden fleece.

Our picture illustrates the scene of Medea's temptation at the fountain. The tempter is love, in the form of Venus, the Greek goddess represented in the old mythology as the inspirer of the tender passion. She is accompanied by the little love-god Cupid, the mischievous fellow whose bow and arrow work so much havoc in human hearts. The perplexed princess sits beside the fountain, holding her head in the attitude of one listening. Venus leans towards her from the other side and softly pleads the lover's cause. Cupid paddles in the water as if quite unconcerned in the affair, but none can tell what mischief he is plotting.

We notice a distinct resemblance between the faces of the two maidens, and perhaps this is the painter's way of telling us that Venus is only Medea's other self: the voice of the tempter speaks from her own heart. The expression is quite different on the two faces, tender and persuasive in Venus, dreamy and preoccupied in Medea. If we turn again to Ovid for the interpretation of the picture, we may fancy that Venus is describing the proud days when, as Jason's bride, Medea would journey with him through the cities of Greece. "My head will touch the very stars with rapture," thought the princess.

The dress of Medea is rich and elegant, but quite simply made; the heavy folds of the skirt describe long, beautiful lines. In one gloved hand she holds a bunch of herbs, and the other rests upon a casket.

The figure of Venus is conceived according to classic tradition, undraped, as the goddess emerged from the sea-foam at her birth. In the Greek religion the human body was honored as a fit incarnation for the deities. Sculptors delighted in the long flowing lines and beautiful curves which could be developed in different poses. Titian's picture translates the spirit of Greek sculpture, so to speak, into the art of painting. The figure of Venus may well be compared with the marble Venus of Milo, in the pure beauty of the face, the exquisite modelling of the figure, and the sweeping lines of grace described in the attitude.[17] The painter contrasts the delicate tint of the flesh with the rich crimson of the mantle which falls from the shoulder.

The landscape is a charming part of the picture, stretching on either side in sunny vistas, pleasantly diversified with woods and waters, hills and pasture lands, church and castle. Sunset lights the sky, and lends its color to the glowing harmonies of the composition.

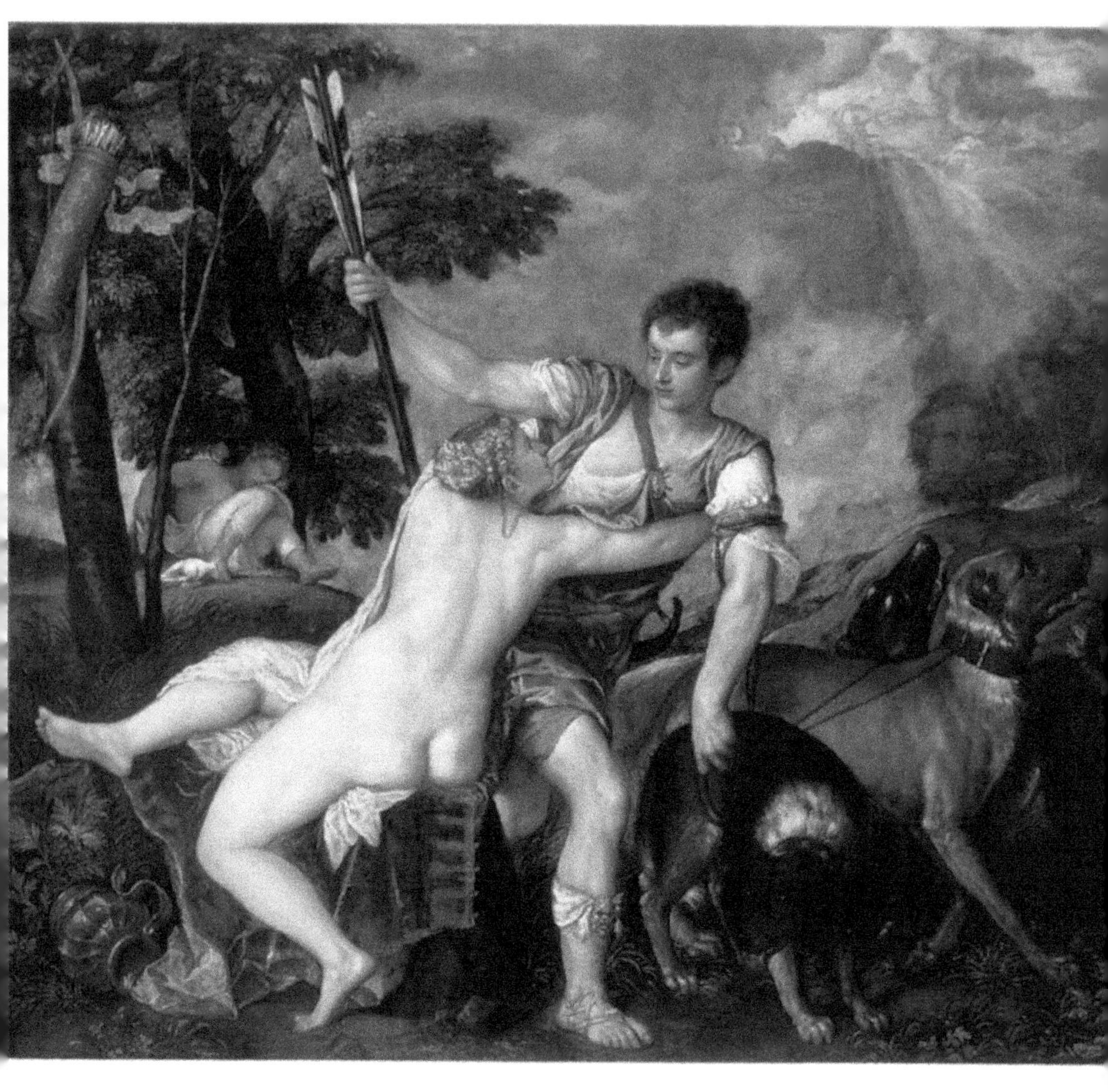

Titian, Venus and Adonis, 1550, Ashmolean, Oxford

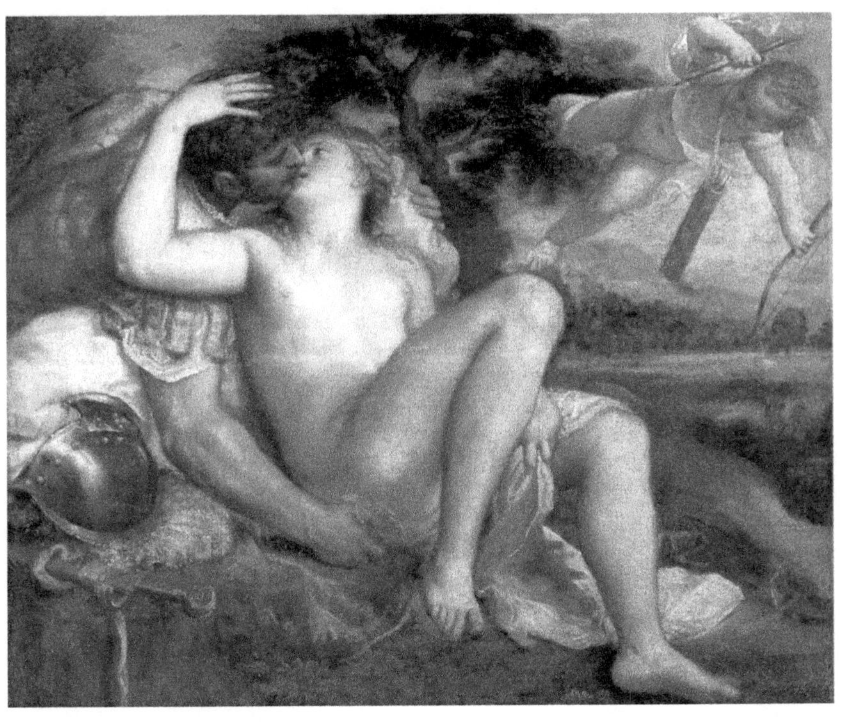

Titian, Venus and Mars and Amor, 1530, Vienna

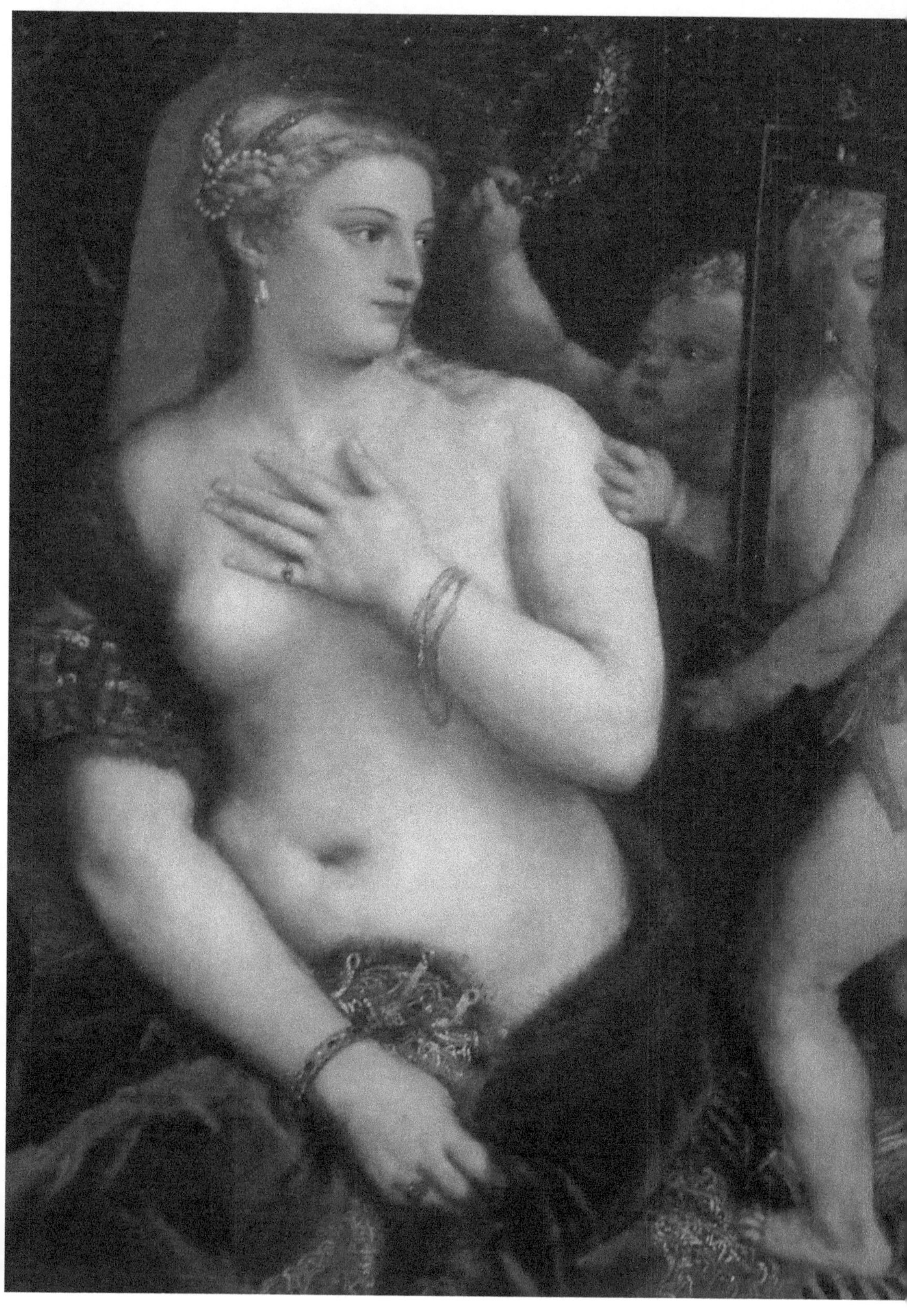

Titian, Venus With a Mirror, 1554-55, Washington, DC

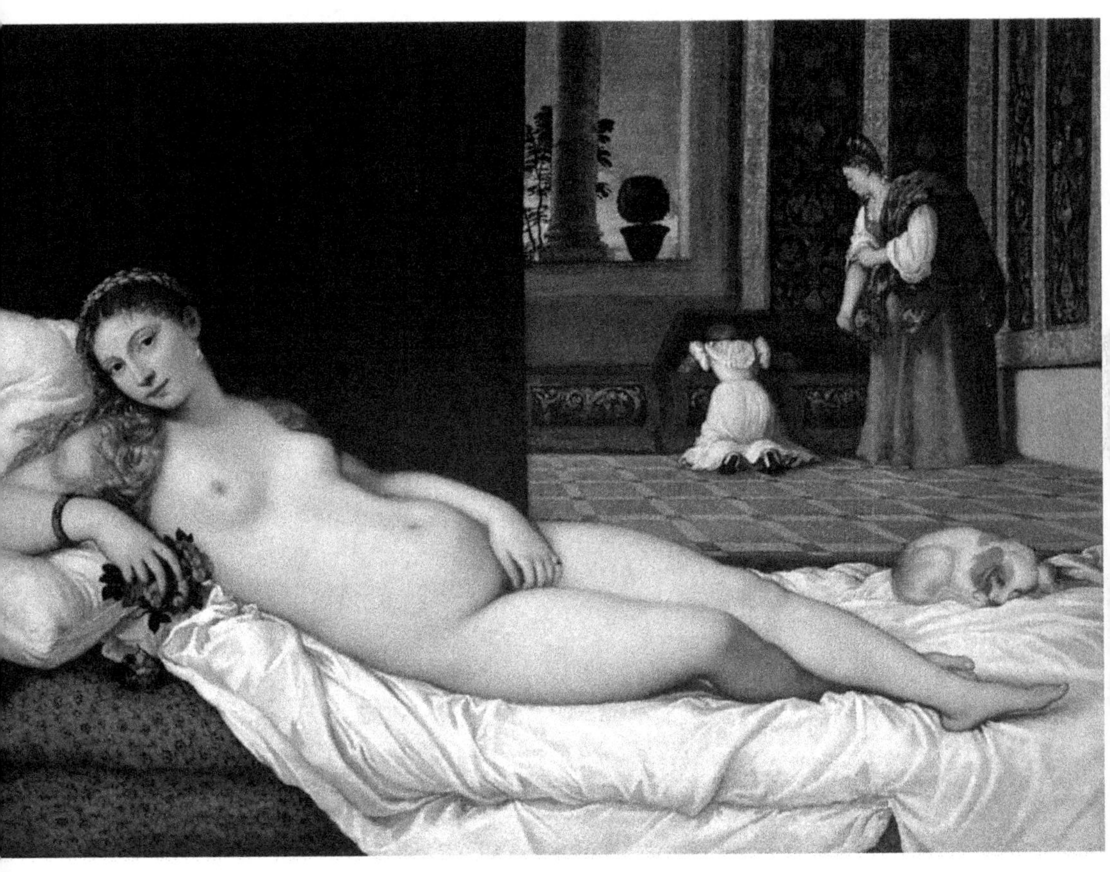

Titian, The Venus of Urbino, 1538, Uffizi, Florence

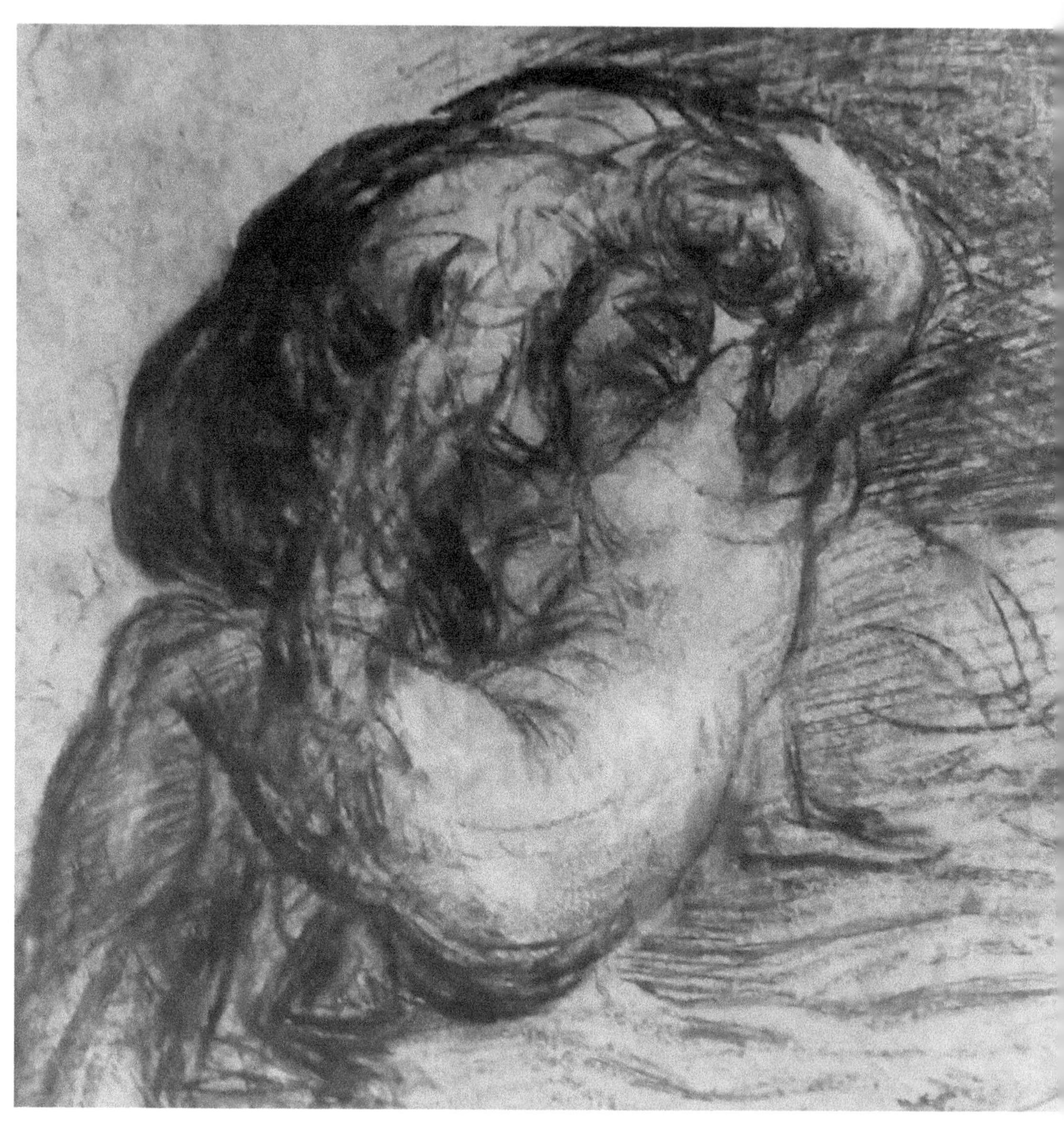

Titian, A Couple, c. 1570, Cambridge

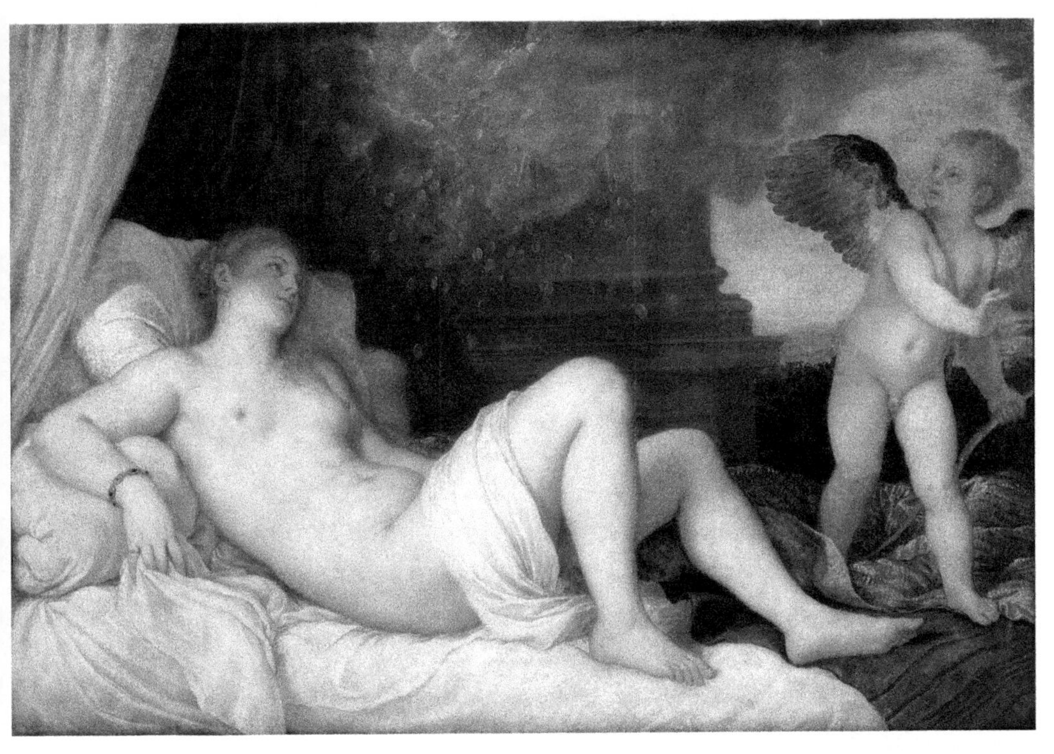

Titian, Danaë, 1544, Naples

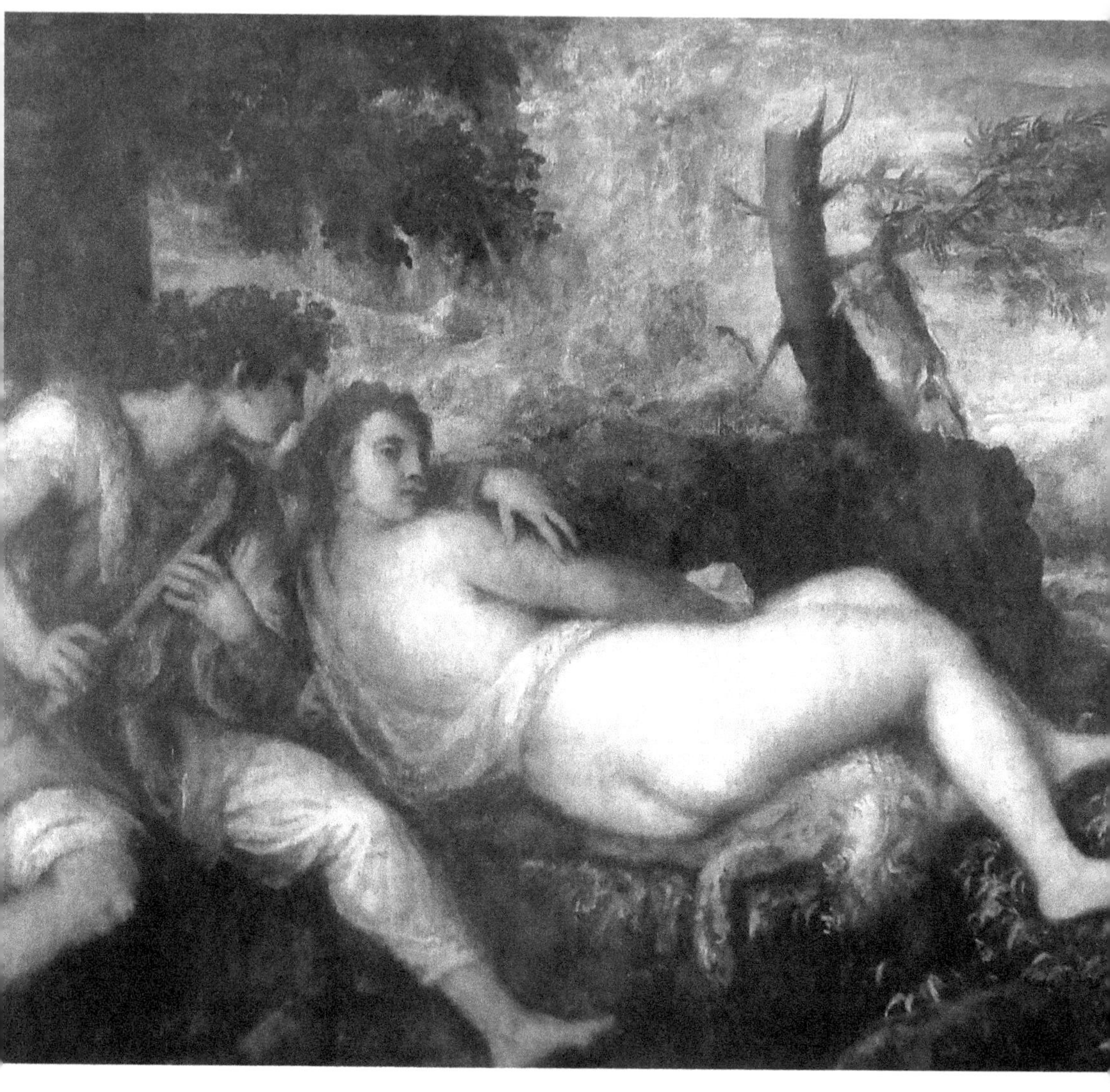

Titian, Nymph and Shepherd, 1575, Vienna

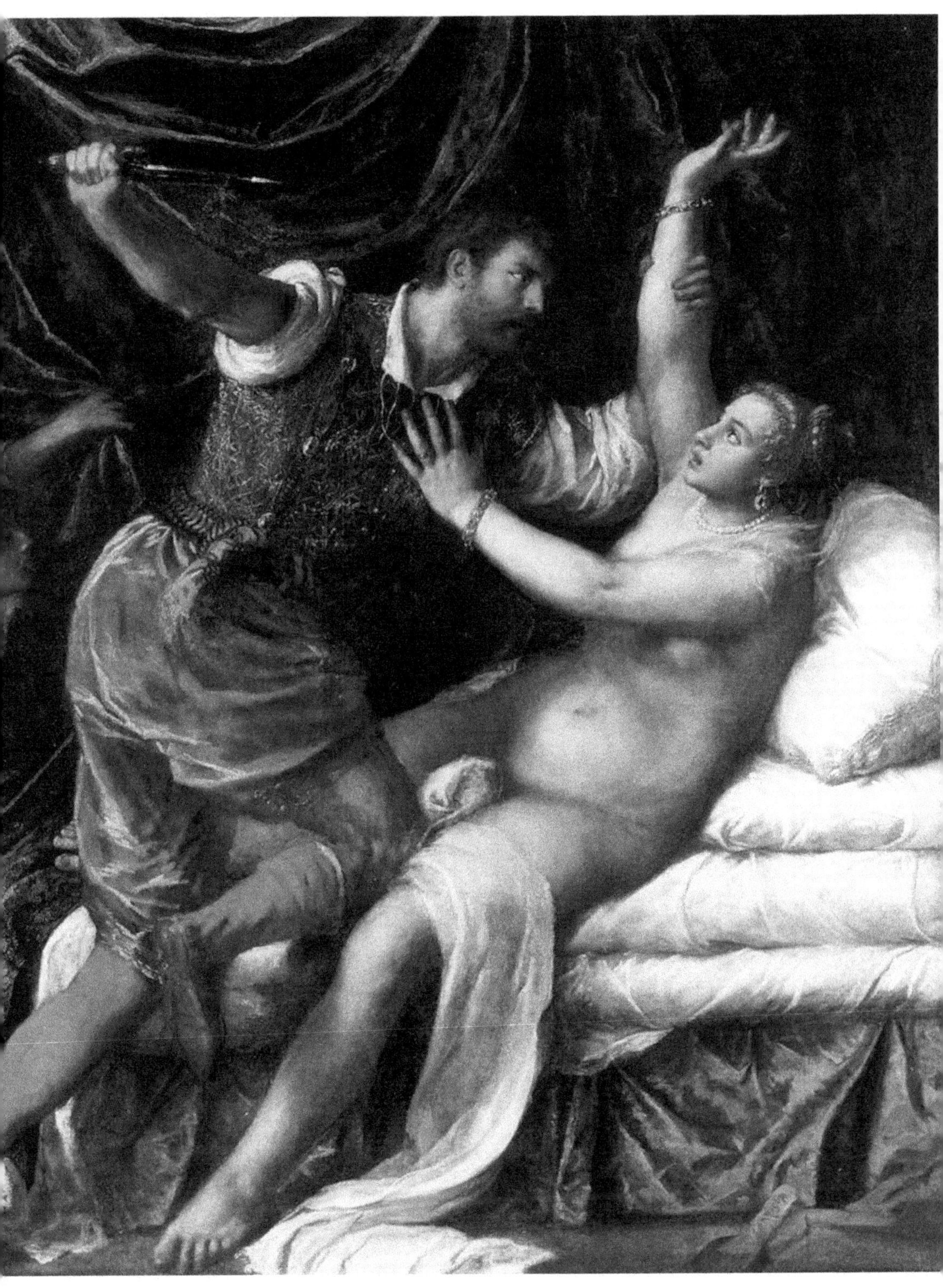

Titian, Tarquin and Lucretia, 1568-71, Cambridge

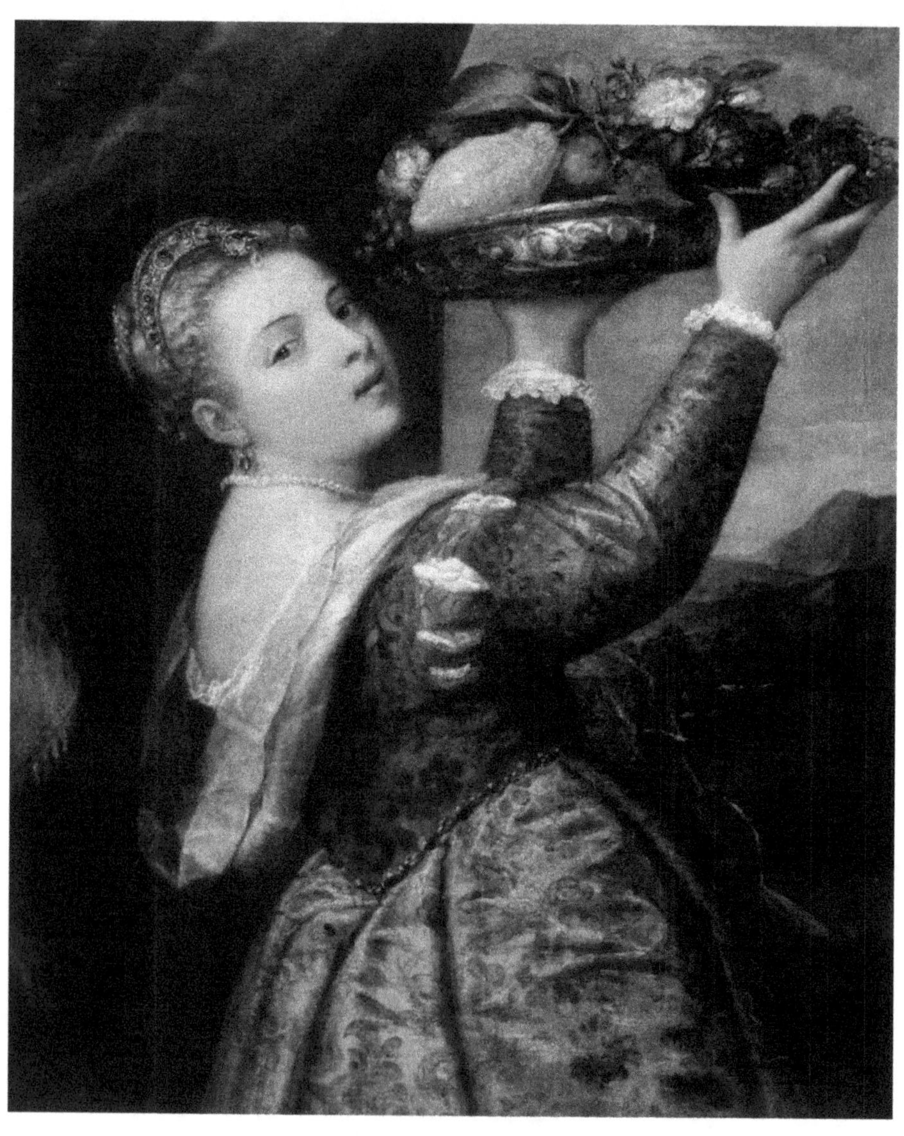

Titian, Girl With a Platter of Fruit, c. 1555, Berlin

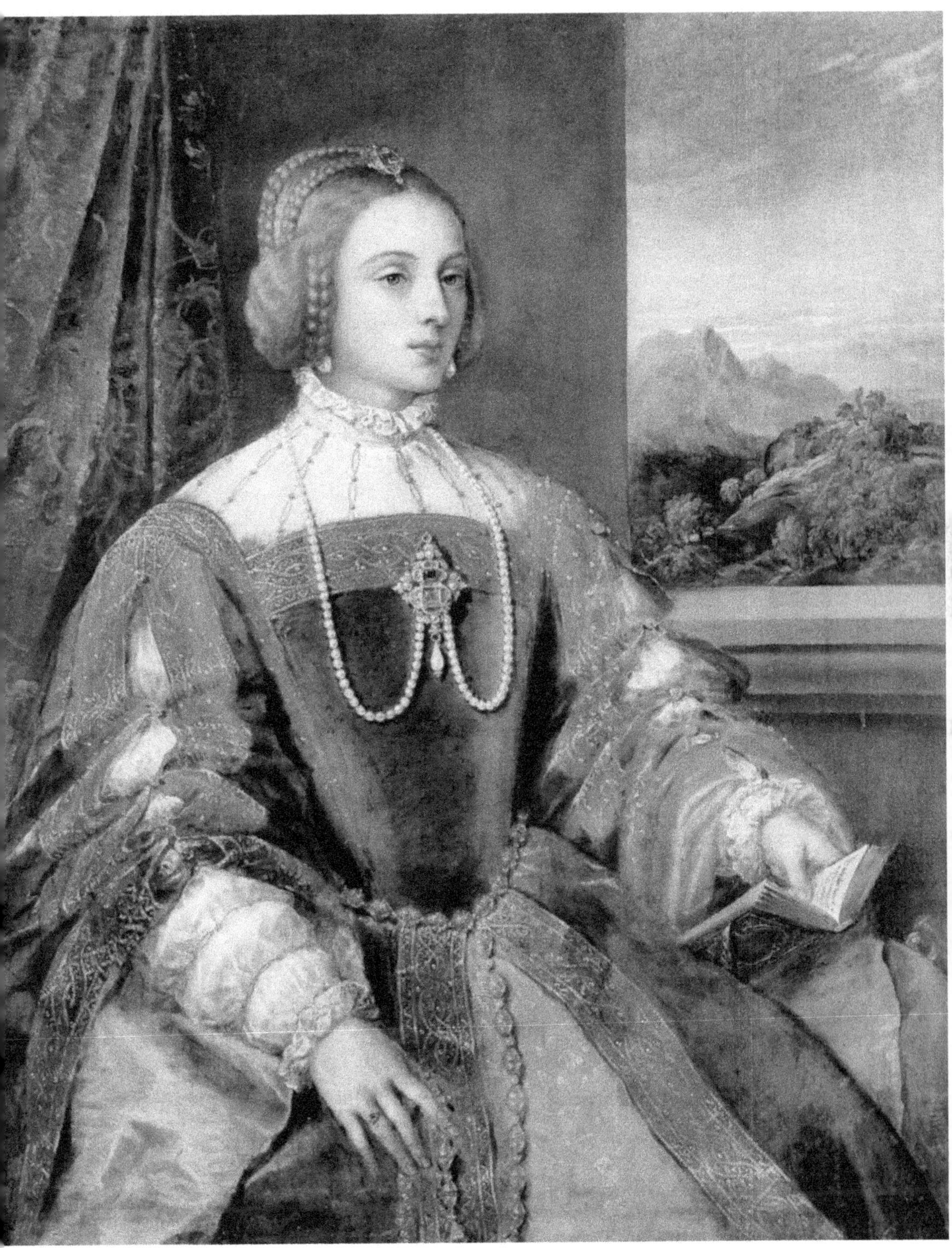

Titian, Portrait of Isabella of Portugal, 1548, Prado

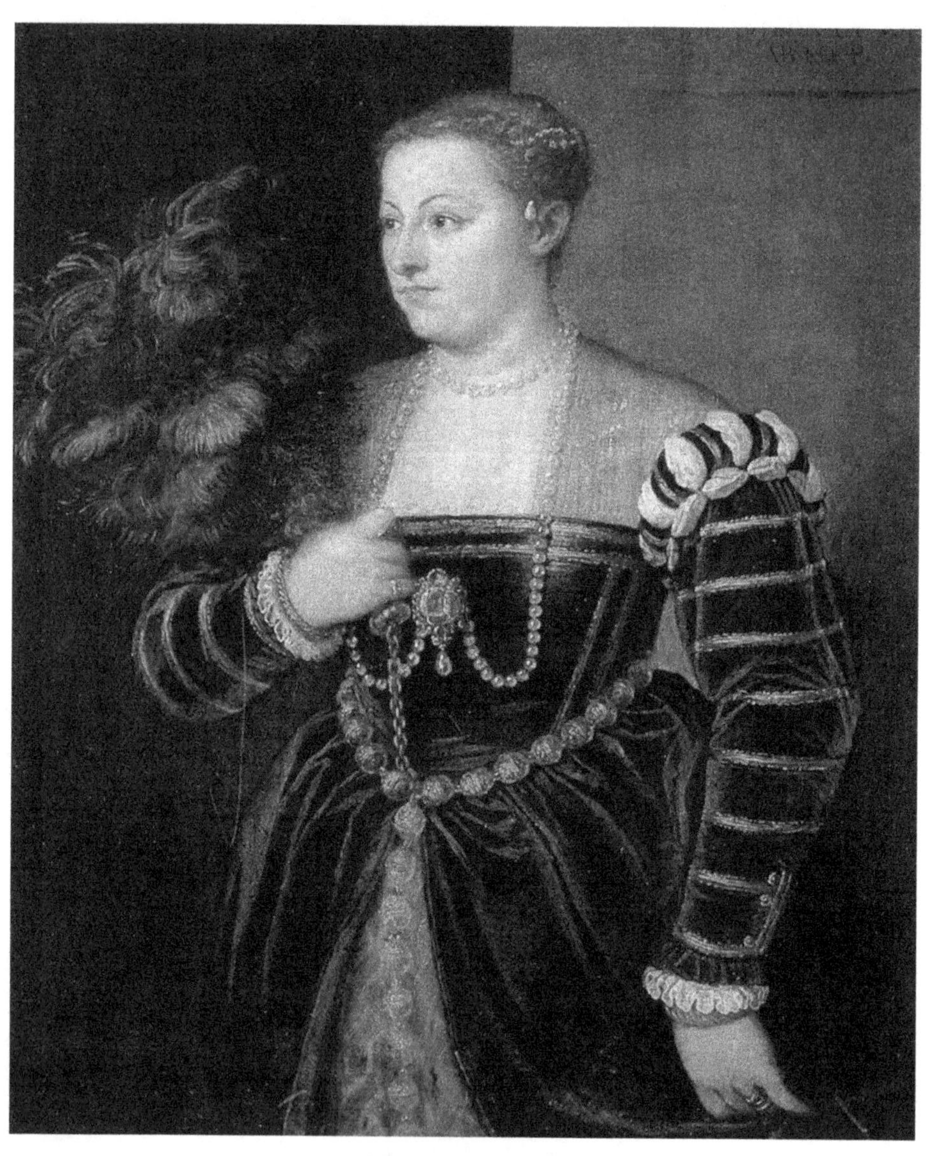

Titian, Lavinia, 1560-65

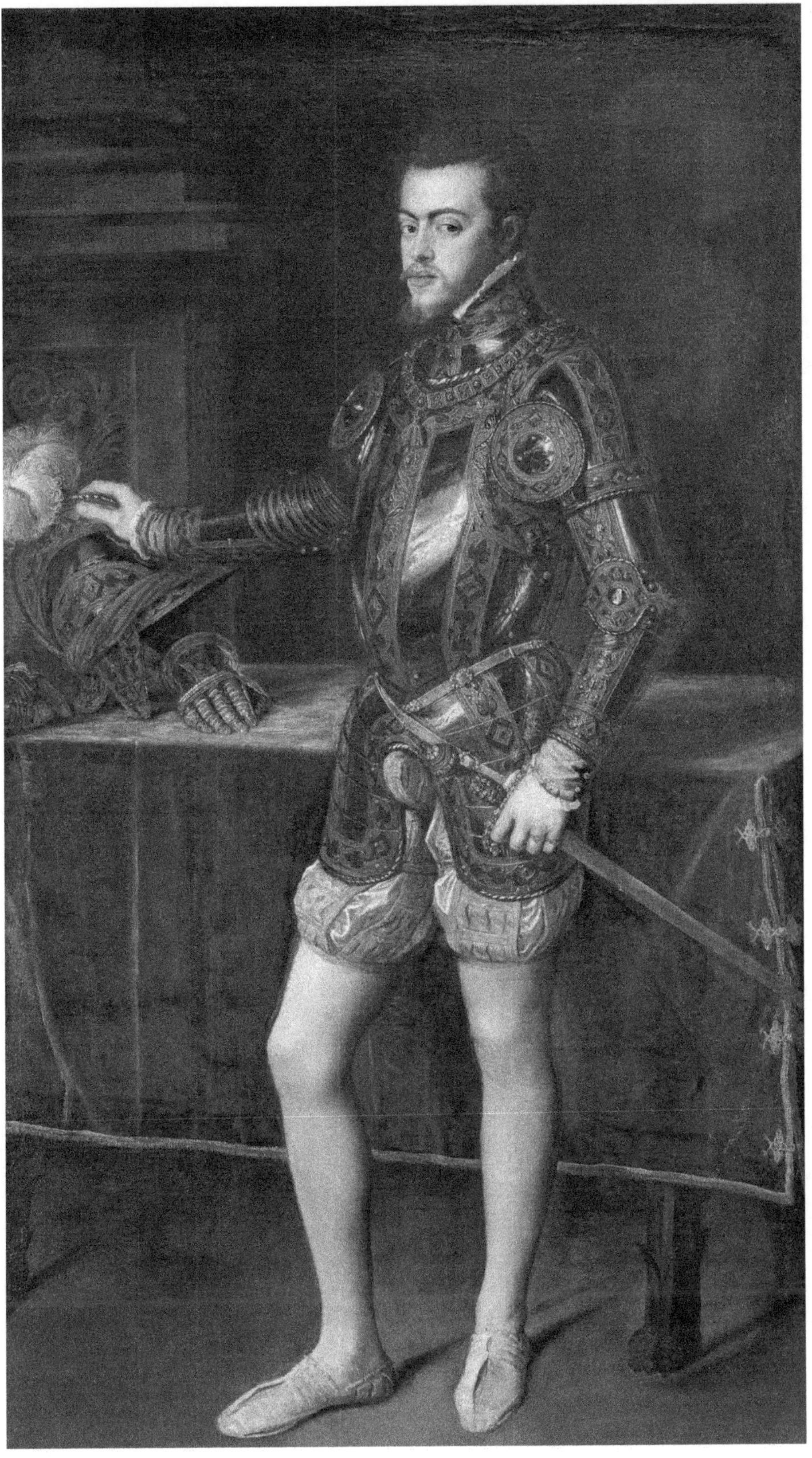

Titian, Philip II, 1551, Prado, Madrid

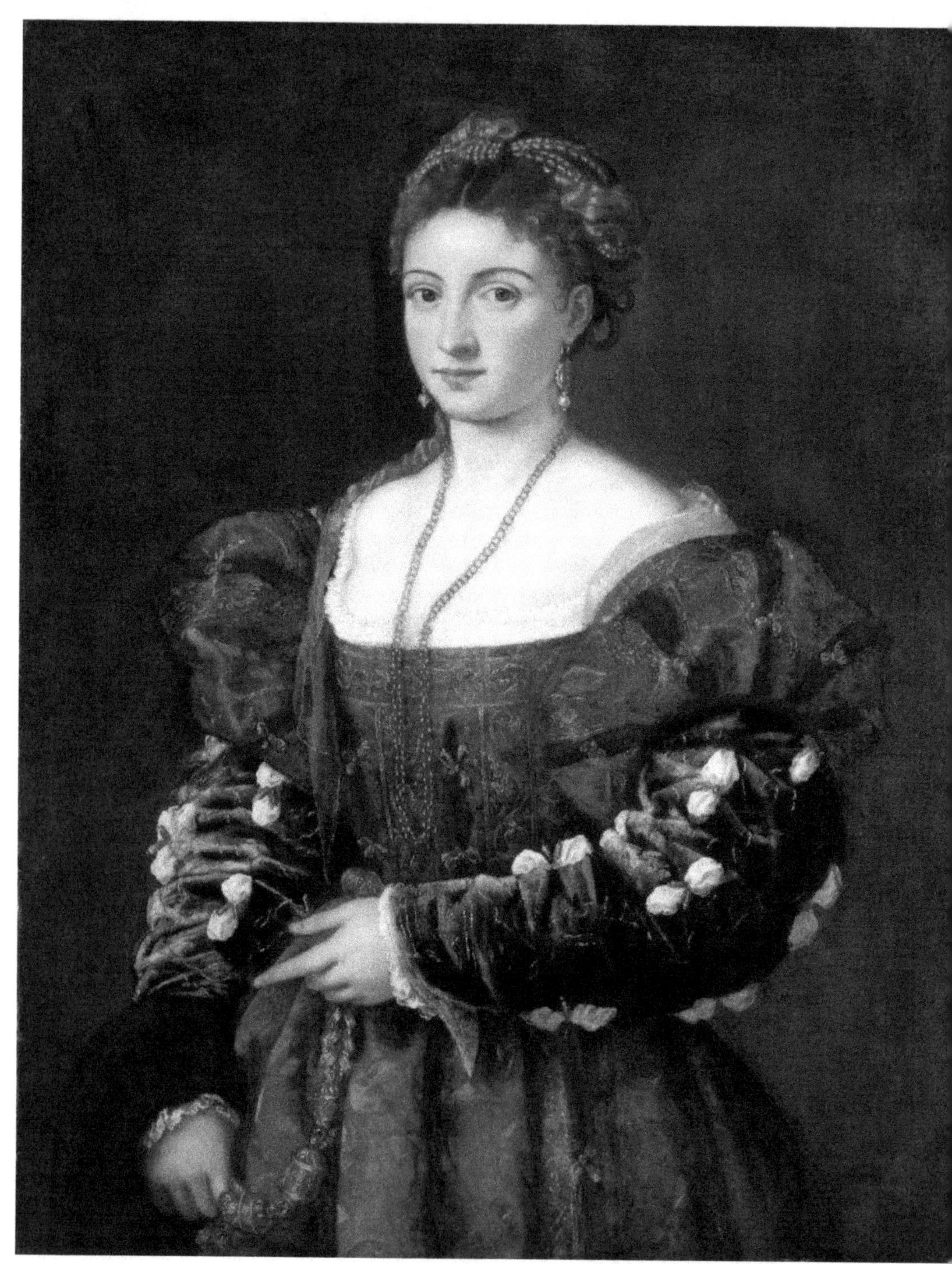

Titian, The Bella, 1536, Pitti Palace

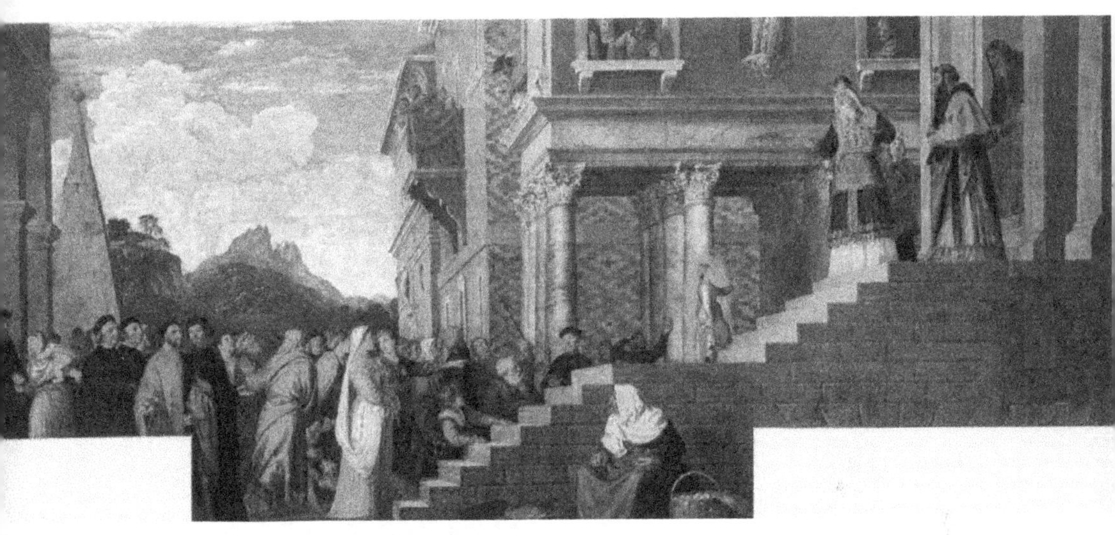

Titian, The Presentation of the Virgin, 1534-38, Venice

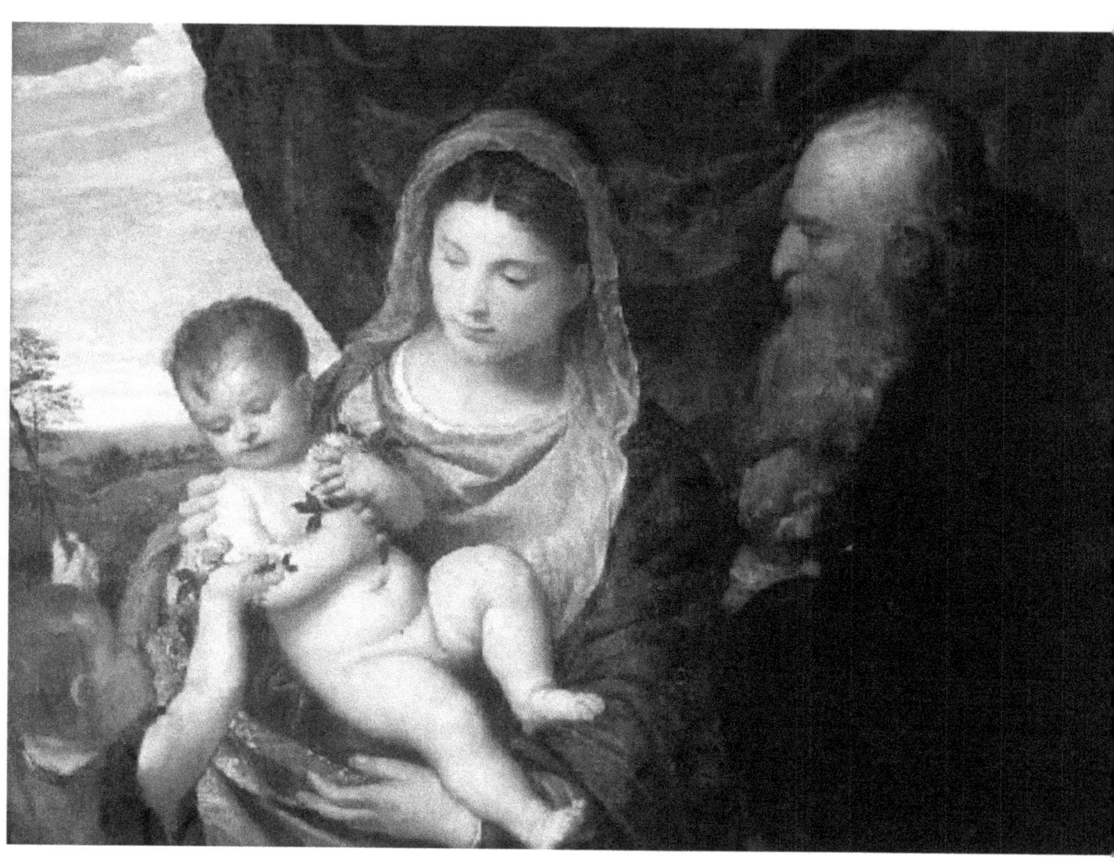

Titian, The Holy Family, 1530s, Uffizi

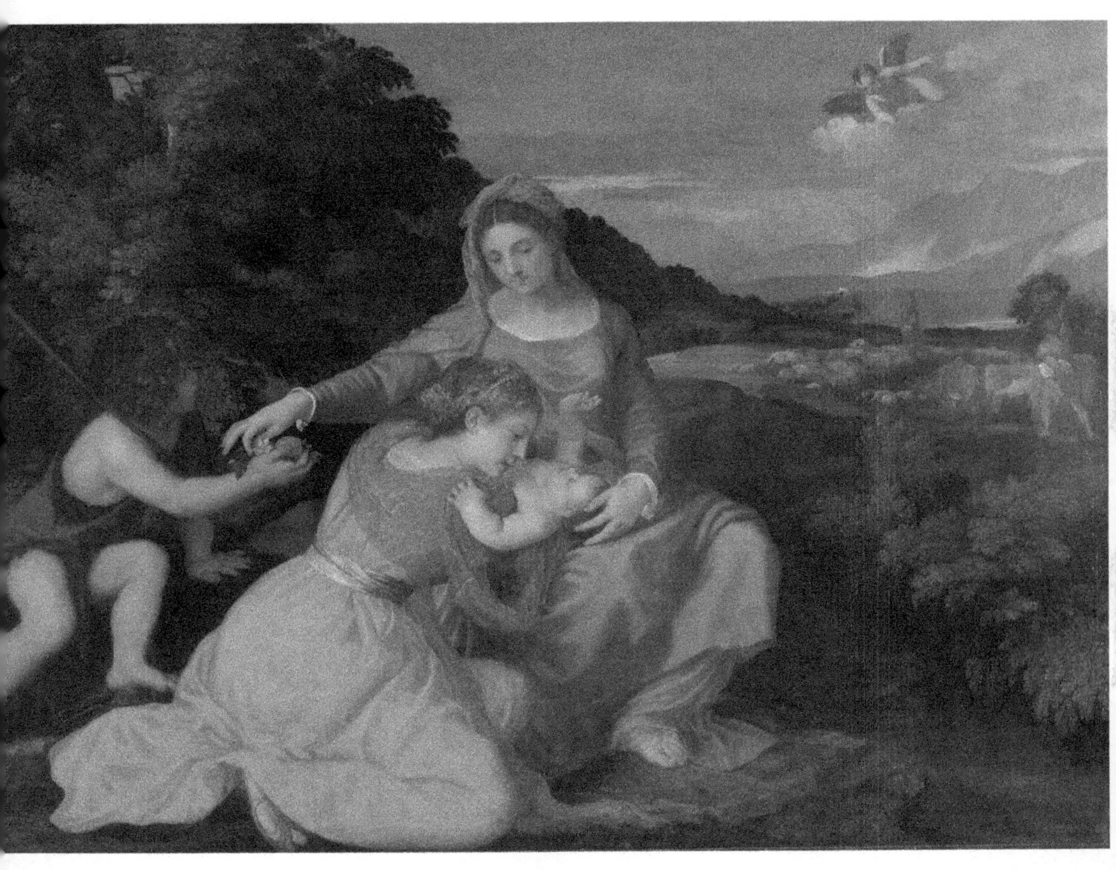

Titian, The Aldobrandini Madonna, National Gallery, London

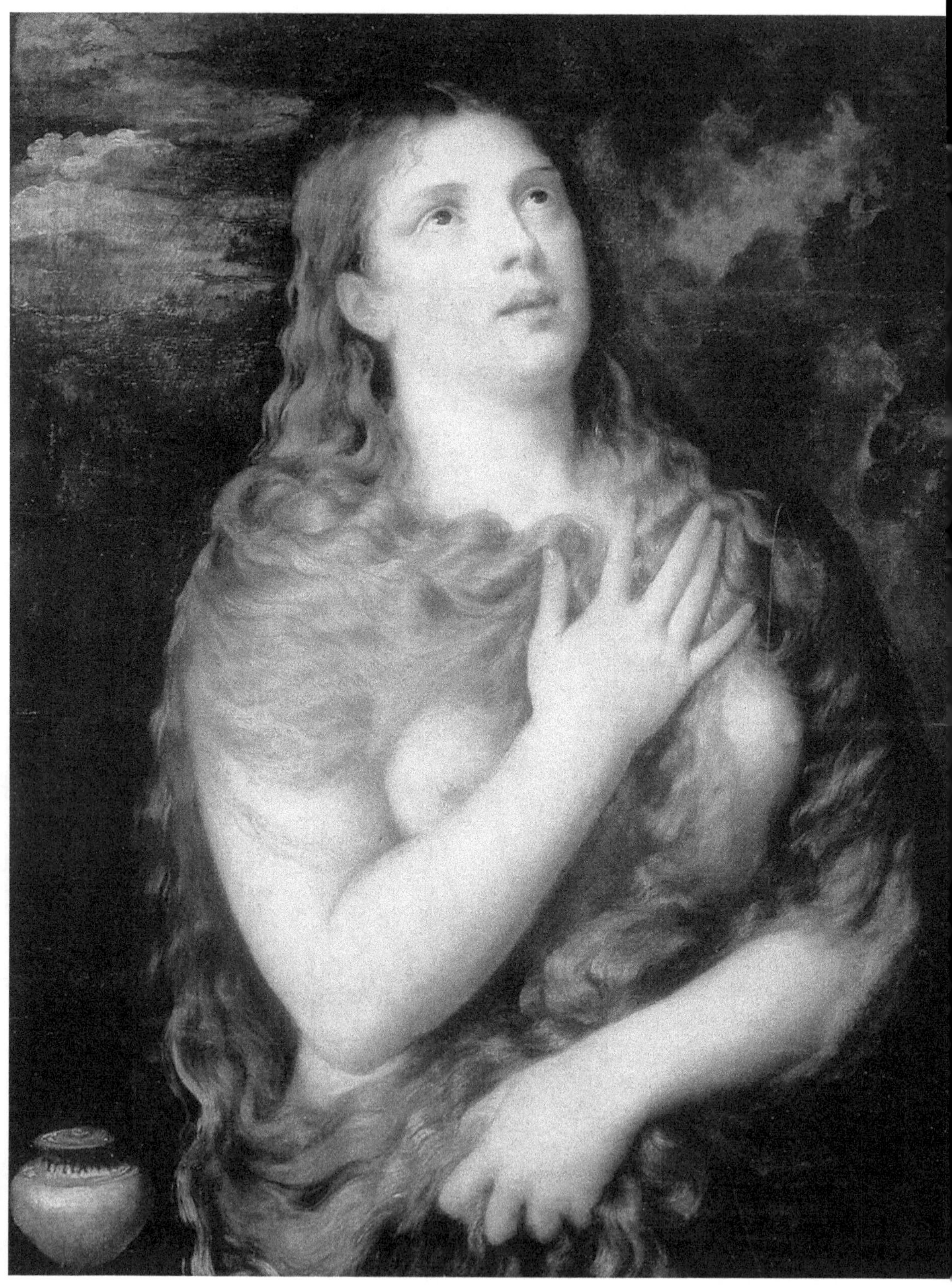

Titian, Mary Magdalene, 1533, Pittit Palace, Florence

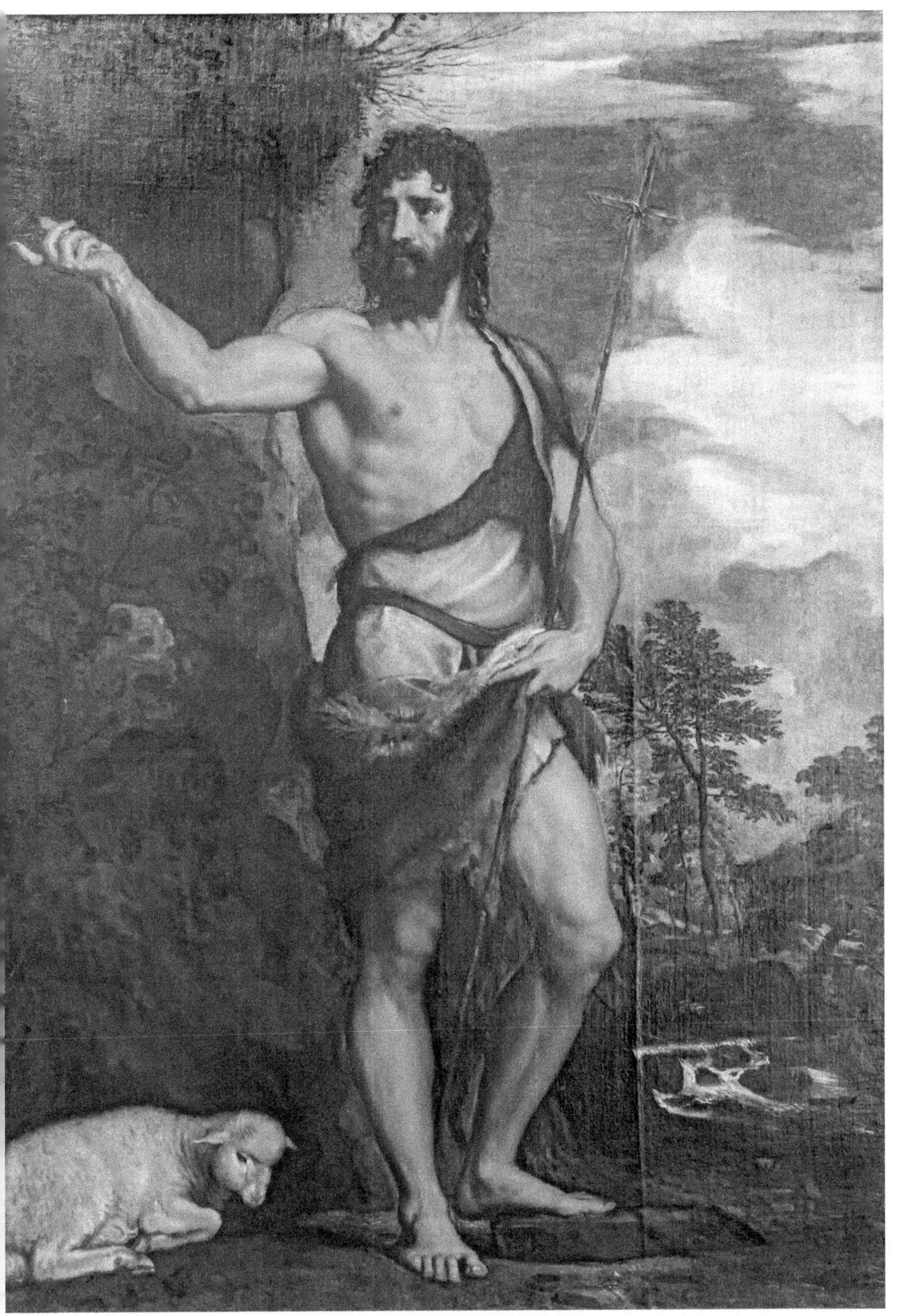

Titian, John the Baptist, 1542, Venice

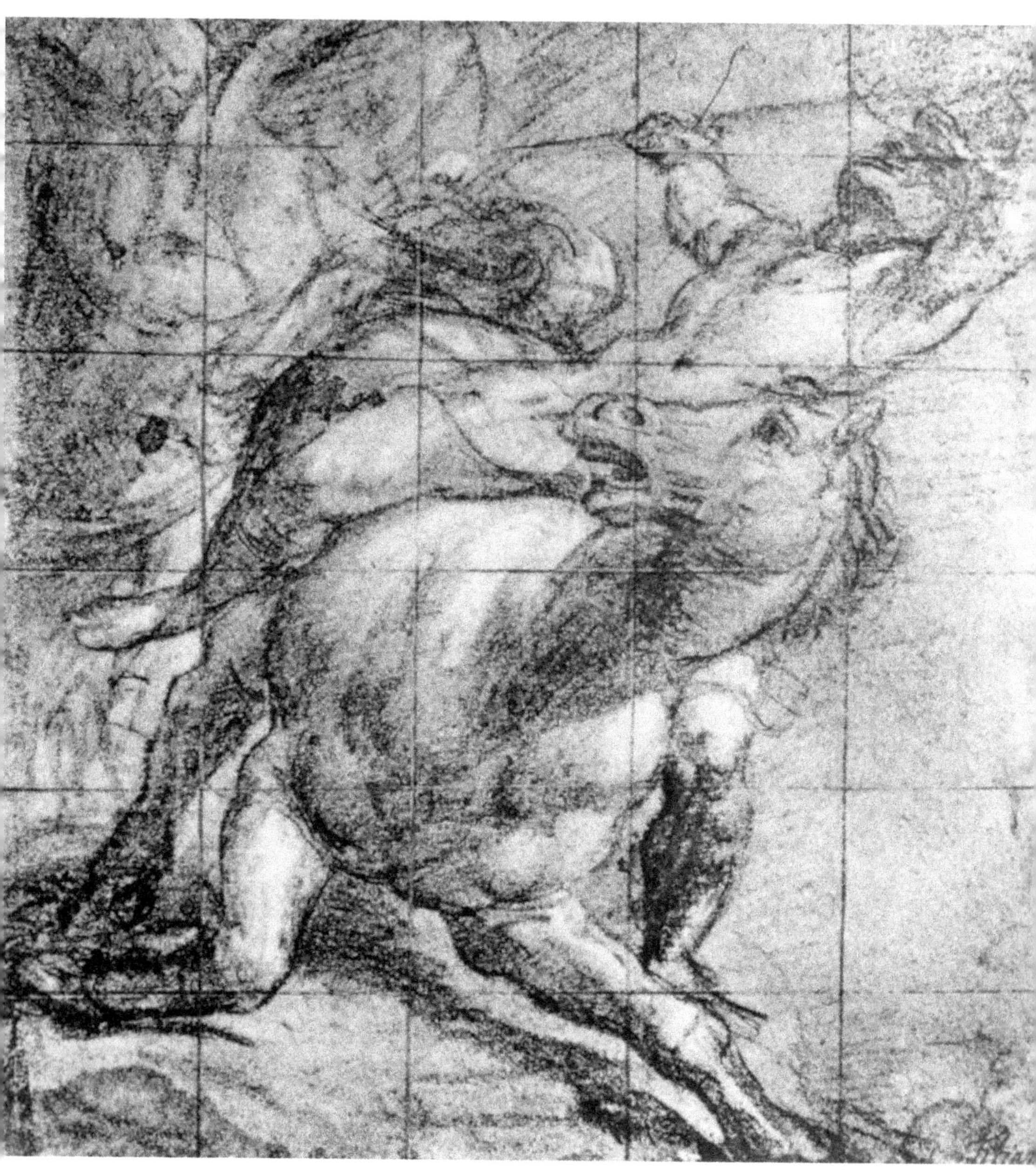

Titian, Studio per cavallo e cavaliere, 1537, Ashmolean Museum, Oxford

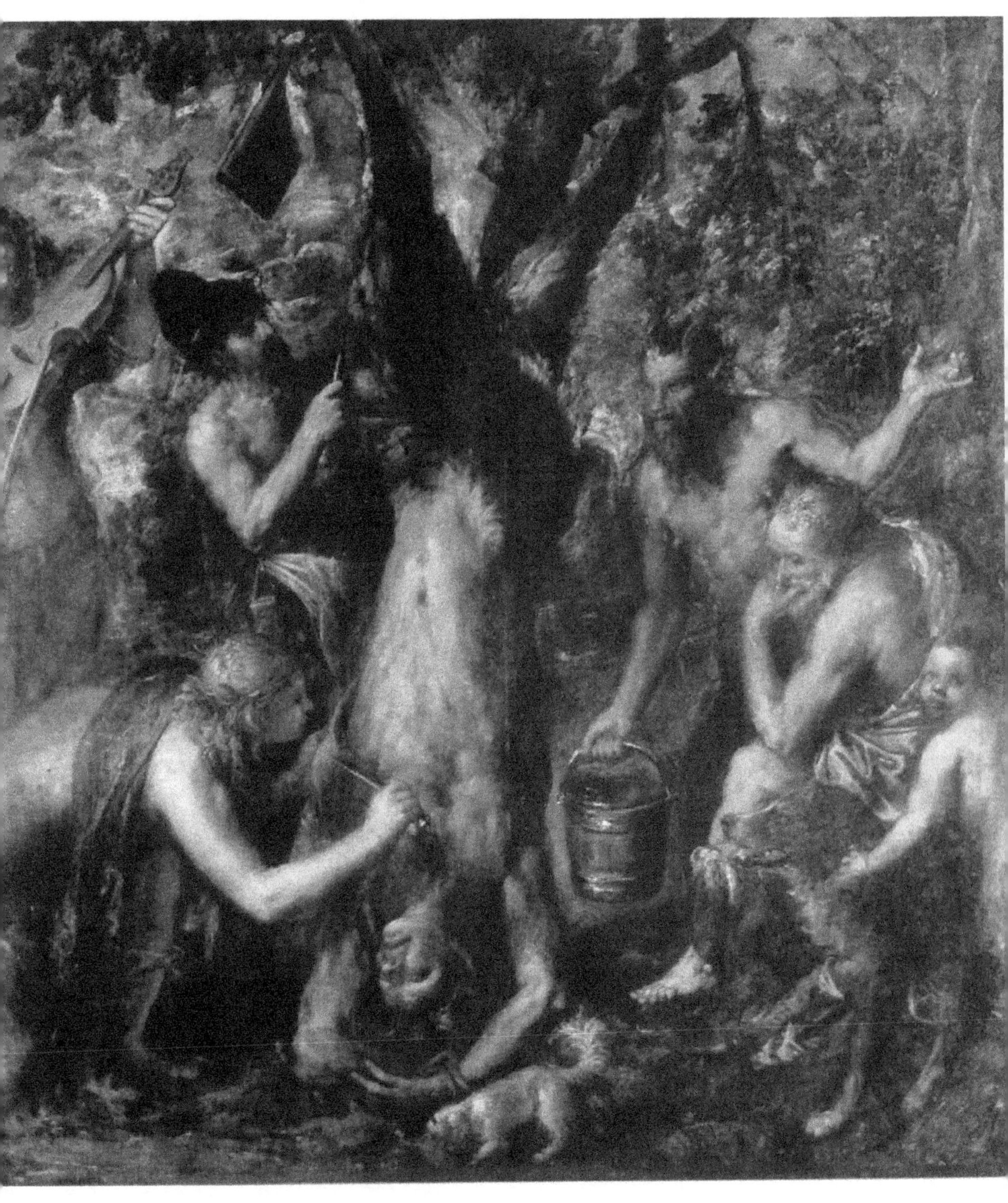

Titian, The Flaying of Marsyas, c. 1570-76, Kromeriz,

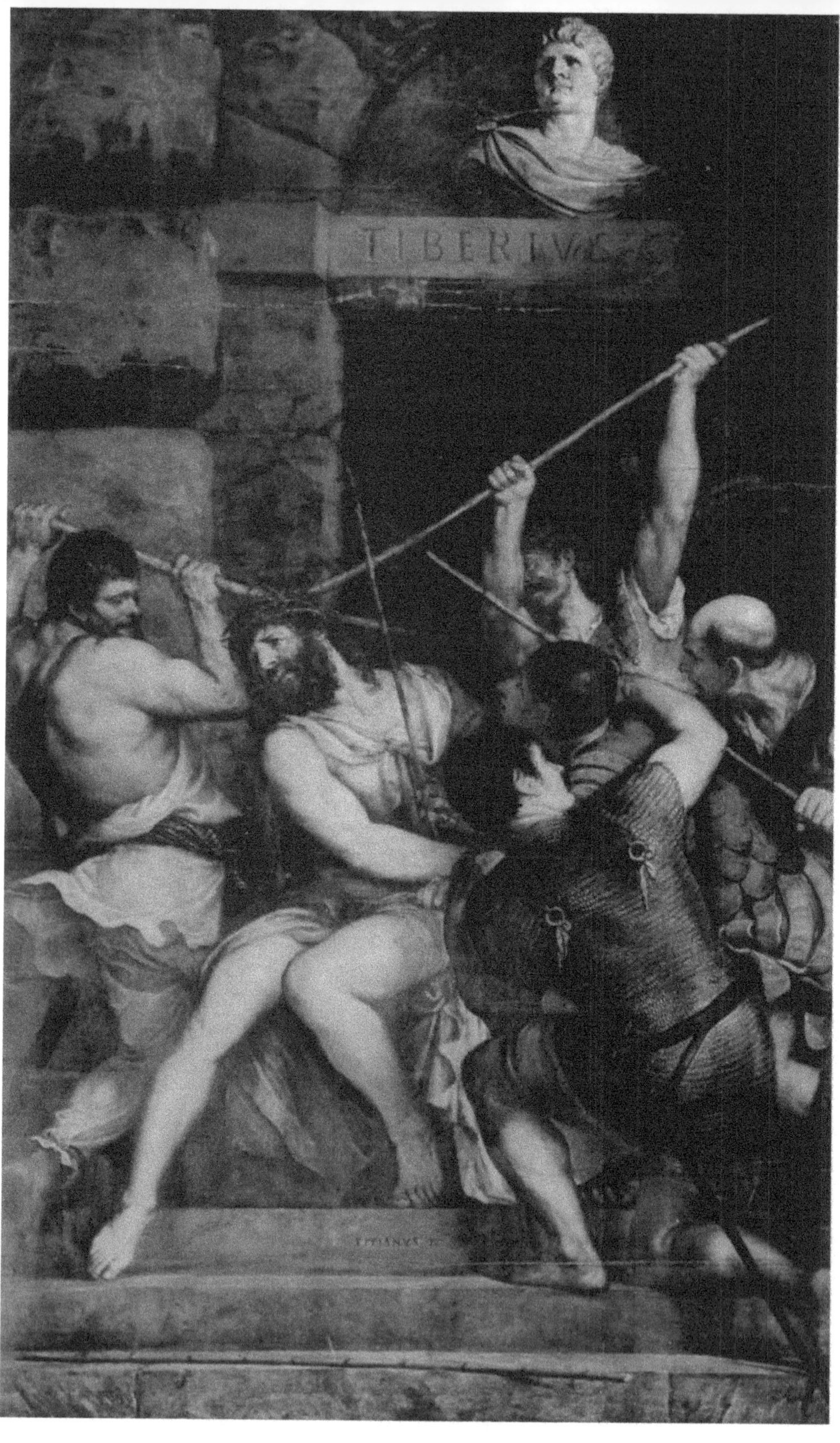

Titian, The Crowning With Thorns, 1572-76, Munich

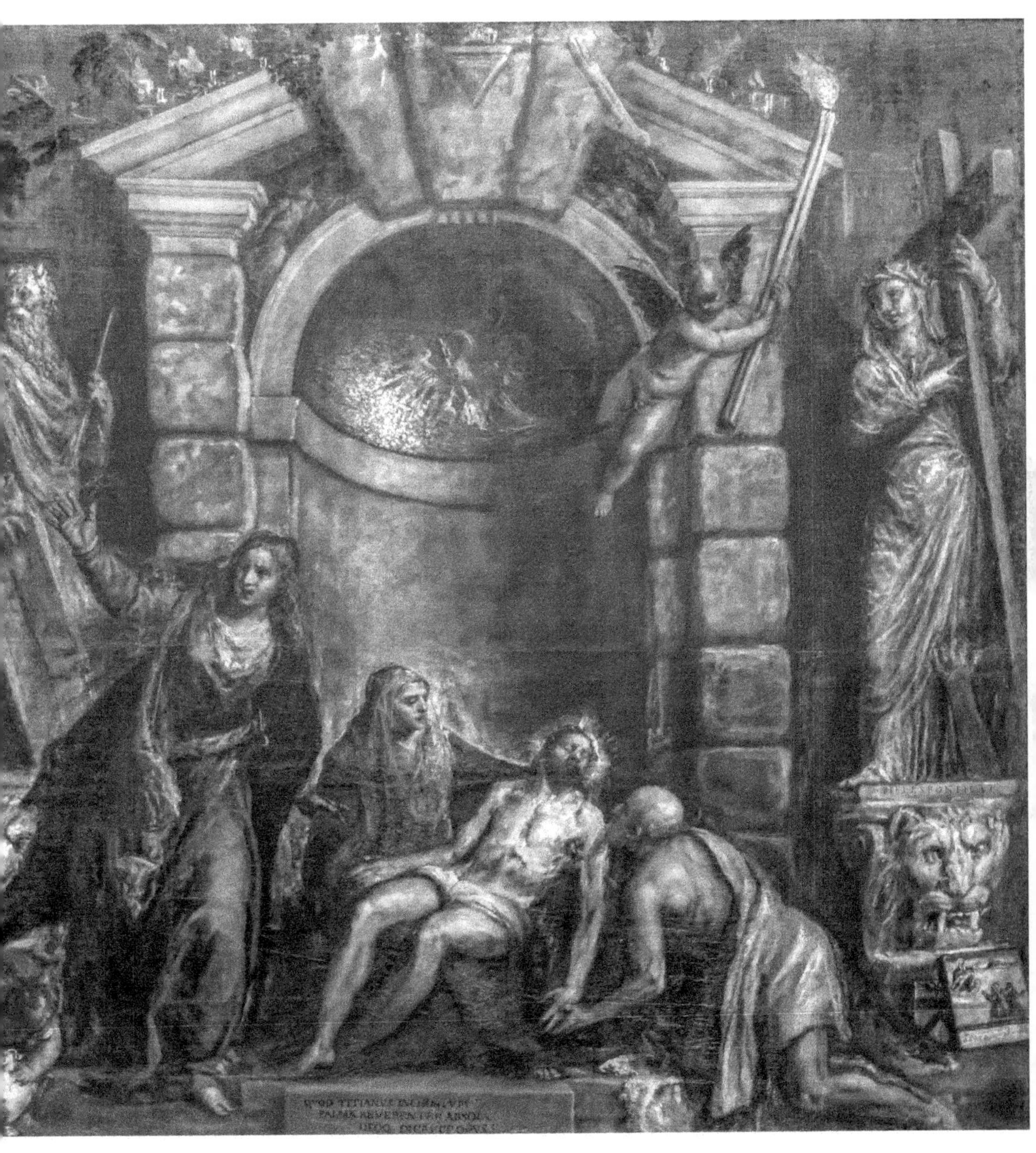

Titian, Pietà, 1576, Venice

XI

THE MAN WITH THE GLOVE

The Man with the Glove is so called for lack of a more definite name. Nothing is told by Titian's biographers about the original of the portrait, and the mystery gives a certain romantic interest to the picture. Not being limited by any actual facts we can invent a story of our own about the person, or as many stories as we like, each according to his fancy.

The sitter certainly makes a good figure for the hero of a romance. He is young and handsome, well dressed, with an unmistakable air of breeding, and singularly expressive eyes. Such eyes usually belong to a shy, sensitive nature, and have a haunting quality like those of some woodland creature.

The title of The Man with the Glove is appropriate in emphasizing an important feature of the costume. In the days of this portrait, gloves were worn only by persons of wealth and distinction, and were a distinguishing mark of elegance. Though somewhat clumsily made, according to our modern notions, they were large enough to preserve the characteristic shape of the hand, and give easy play to the fingers. They formed, too, a poetic element in the social life of the age of chivalry. It was by throwing down his glove (or gauntlet) that one knight challenged another; while a glove was also sometimes a love-token between a knight and his lady.

The glove has its artistic purpose in the picture, casting the left hand into shadow, to contrast with the ungloved right hand. The texture of the leather is skilfully rendered, and harmonizes pleasantly with the serious color scheme of the composition.

Besides the gloves, the daintily ruffled shirt, the seal ring, and the long neck chain, show the sitter to be a young man of fashion. Not that he is in the least a fop, but he belongs to that station in life where fine raiment is a matter of course, and he wears it as one to the manner born. His hands are delicately modelled, but they are not the plump hands of an idler. They are rather flexible and sensitive, with long fingers like the hands of an artist.

The glossy hair falls over the ears, and is brushed forward and cut in a straight line across the forehead. The style suits well the open frankness of the countenance. We must note Titian's rendering of both hair and hands as points of excellence in the portrait. There is a great deal of individuality in the texture of a person's hair and the shape of his hands, but many artists have apparently overlooked this fact. Van Dyck, for instance, used a model who furnished the hands for his portraits, irrespective of the sitter. Titian, in his best work, counted nothing too trivial for faithful artistic treatment.

If we were to try to explain why The Man with the Glove is a great work of art we should find the first reason, perhaps, in the fact that the man seems actually alive. The portrait has what the critics call vitality, in a remarkable degree. Again, the painter has revealed in the face the inner life of the man himself; the portrait is a revelation of his personality.

It has been said that every man wears an habitual mask in the presence of his fellows. It is only when he is taken unaware that the mask drops, and the man's real self looks out of his face. The portrait painter's art must catch the sitter's expression in such a moment of unconsciousness. The great artist must be a seer as well as a painter, to penetrate the secrets of human character.

The young man of our picture is one of those reticent natures capable of intense feeling. In this moment of unconsciousness his very soul seems to look forth from his eyes. It is the soul of a poet, though he may not possess the gift of song. He has the poet's imagination as a dreamer of noble dreams.

The time seems to have come when he is just awakening to the possibilities of life. He faces the future seriously, but with no shrinking. One recalls the words of Gareth, in Tennyson's Idyll:

"Man am I grown, a man's work must I do.
•
Live pure, speak true, right wrong, follow the king -
Else wherefore born?"[18]

The lofty ideals of the knights of King Arthur's Round Table are such as we feel sure this gentle spirit would make his own:-

"To reverence the king as if he were
Their conscience, and their conscience as their king,
To break the heathen and uphold the Christ,
To ride abroad redressing human wrongs,
To speak no slander, no nor listen to it,
To lead sweet lives in purest chastity,
To love one maiden only, cleave to her,
And worship her by years of noble deeds
Until they won her."[19]

It may be of these "noble deeds" of chivalry that our young man is dreaming, or it may be of that "one maiden " for whose sake they are to be done. Certainly these candid eyes see visions which we should be glad to see, and show us the depths of a knightly soul.

XII

THE ASSUMPTION OF THE VIRGIN

The Virgin Mary, mother of Jesus, has for over nineteen centuries represented to Christendom all the ideal qualities of womanhood. In her character, as revealed in St. Luke's gospel, we read of her noble, trustful humility in accepting the message of the Annunciation; of her decision and prudence shown in her visit to Elizabeth; of her intellectual power as manifested in the song of the Magnificat; of the contemplative nature with which she watched the growth of Jesus; of her maternal devotion throughout her son's ministry, - and of her sublime fortitude and faith at his crucifixion.[20] Such was the woman so highly favored of God, she whom the angel called "blessed among women."

Art has pictured for us many imaginary scenes from the life of Mary. The most familiar and best loved subject is that of her motherhood, where she is seen with her babe in her arms. There are other subjects, less common, showing her as a glorified figure in mid-air as in a vision. One such is that called the Immaculate Conception, which the Spanish painter Murillo so frequently repeated.[21] Another is the Assumption, representing her at her death as borne by angels to heaven.

The "Golden Legend " relates how " the right fair among the daughters of Jerusalem ... full of charity and dilection" was "joyously received" into glory. "The angels were glad, the archangels enjoyed, the thrones sang, the dominations made melody, the principalities harmonized, the potestates harped, cherubim and seraphim sang laudings and praisings." Also, "the angels were with the apostles singing, and replenished all the land with marvelous sweetness."

The Assumption of the Virgin is the subject of a noble painting by Titian, one of the most celebrated pictures in the world. A group of apostles stand on the earth gazing after the receding figure of the Virgin as she soars into the air on a wreath of cloud-borne angels. From the upper air the Heavenly Father floats downward with his angels to receive her. As the canvas is very large, over twenty-two feet in height, a small reproduction of the entire picture is unsatisfactory, and our illustration gives us the heart of the composition for careful study.

The Virgin rises buoyantly through the air, and the figure is so full of life and motion that it seems as if it would presently soar beyond our sight. The heavy folds of the skirt swirl about the body in the swiftness of the ascent. The rushing air fills the mantle like the sail of a ship. Yet the source of motion is not within the figure itself, for we see the feet resting firmly on the cloud. It is as if she were borne aloft in a celestial chariot composed of an angelic host.

The face is lifted with a look of rapture; the arms are extended in a gesture of exultation. The pose of the head displays the beautiful throat, strong and full like that of a singer. The features are cast in a large, majestic mould. The hands, turned palm outward, are large and flexible, but with delicate, tapering fingers.

We have already seen in other pictures what was Titian's conception of the Virgin in her girlhood and motherhood. We find little of the ethereal and spiritual in his ideal, and nothing that would in any way suggest that true piety is morbid or sentimental. Other painters have erred in this direction, but not Titian. To him the Virgin was no angel in disguise, but a strong, happy, healthy woman, rejoicing in life. But though a woman, she was in the poet's phrase "a woman above all women glorified." She possessed in perfection all the good gifts of human nature. Titian's ideal coincided with the old Greek formula, "A sound mind in a sound body." The Virgin of the Assumption is in fact not unlike a Greek goddess in her magnificently developed physique and glorious beauty.

Our illustration includes a few of the baby angels from the wreath supporting the Madonna. They are packed so closely together in the picture that their little limbs interlace like interwoven stems in a garland of flowers. Yet the figures are cunningly arranged to bring into prominence a series of radiating lines which flow towards a centre in the Madonna's face. We see in the corner of our print a little arm pointing to the Virgin, and above it is a cherub's wing drawn in the same oblique line.

Frolicsome as is this whole company of angels, they are of an almost unearthly beauty. A poetic critic has told of standing before the picture contemplating these lovely spirits one after another, until, as she expresses it, "A thrill came over me like that which I felt when Mendelssohn played the organ and I became music while I listened." She sums up the effect of the picture as "mind and music and love, kneaded, as it were, into form and color." [22]

When we analyze the drawing of the Madonna's figure we see that it is drawn in an outline of long, beautiful curves. The principle of repetition is skilfully worked into the composition. The outer sleeve falls away from the right arm in an oval which exactly duplicates that made by the lower portion of the mantle sweeping out at one side. By tracing the main lines of the drapery one will find them running in parallels.

XIII

FLORA

Besides the portraits intended as actual likenesses of the sitters, Titian was fond of painting what may be called ideal portraits, or fancy pictures. While real persons furnished the original models for these, the painter let his imagination have free play in modifying and perfecting form and feature. We have seen an illustration of this process in the picture called the Bella, an idealized portrait of Eleanora Gonzaga. The Flora is another example.

We do not know the name of the original, but we may be sure that it represents an actual person. There is a tradition that she was the daughter of one of Titian's fellow-painters, Palma, with whom he was in love. As a matter of fact, Palma had no daughter, and the young woman was doubtless only a favorite Venetian model whom both painters employed. Apparently it was she who posed for both figures in the picture of Medea and Venus which we have studied.[23]

Flora's hair is of that auburn tint which the Venetians loved, and which, it is believed, was artificially produced. It is looped into soft, waving puffs over the ears, and gathered back by a silken cord, below which it falls like a delicate veil thinly spread over the shoulders. The skin is exquisitely white and soft, and the thin garment has been allowed to slip from one shoulder so that we may see the full, beautiful neck.

We notice with what art the painter has arranged the draperies. From the right shoulder the garment falls in delicate, radiating folds across the figure. Over the garment is thrown a stiff, rose-colored brocade mantle, contrasting pleasantly with the former both in color and texture. A glimpse of this mantle is seen at the right side and above the left shoulder and arm, over which the hand gathers it up to prevent it from slipping. This action of the left hand introduces a new set of lines into the picture, breaking the folds of the drapery into eddying circles which offset the more sweeping lines of the composition. [24]

The drawing here is well worth studying, and we may give it more attention since we must lose the lovely color of the painting in the reproduction. The main lines flow in diagonals in two opposite directions. There is the long line of the right arm and shoulder drawn in a fine, strong curve across the canvas. Parallel with it is the edge of the brocade mantle as it is held in the left hand. The counter lines are the curve of the neck and left shoulder, with which the upper edge of the undergarment runs parallel. The wide spaces between these enclosing lines are broken by sprays of radiating lines, one formed by the folds of the undergarment, and the other smaller one by the locks of hair on the left shoulder.

The graceful pose of the head, inclined to one side, suggests the soft languor of a southern temperament. It was often adopted by Titian, and we see another instance in the attitude of the Venus. We fancy that the painters liked particularly the long curve thus obtained along the neck and shoulder. The angle made on the other side between head and shoulder is filled in with the falling hair.

The title of Flora is given to the picture after the fashion of Titian's time for drawing subjects from mythology. The revival of classic learning had opened to Italian art a delightful new field of illustration. We see how Titian took advantage of it in such pictures as Medea and Venus. In England the love of the classics was seen in the poetry which took much the same place there that painting held in Italy. Flora was the ancient goddess of flowers and is made much of in Elizabethan verse. [25] Some pretty lines by Richard Carlton describe

> "When Flora fair the pleasant tidings bringeth
> Of summer sweet with herbs and flowers adorned."

In our picture the goddess holds a handful of flowers, roses, jessamine and violets, as a sign of her identity. We confess that her type of beauty hardly corresponds to our ideal of Flora. She is a gentle, amiable creature, but not ethereal and poetic enough for the goddess of flowers. Were we to choose a character for her from mythology it would be Juno, the matronly "ox-eyed" goddess, who presided over marriage and whose emblem was the productive pomegranate.

As we compare Flora with the other fair women of our collection, we see that her beauty is of a less elegant and aristocratic type than that of the Bella, and less delicate and refined than that of the Empress Isabella. Her face is perhaps too broad to satisfy a connoisseur of beauty, and she is quite plainly of plebeian caste. Like Lavinia her charm is in the healthy vitality which was the special characteristic of the Venetian beauties of the time. The figure glows with warm pulsing life.

XIV

THE PESARO MADONNA

High on a great marble pedestal, between the stately pillars of a temple, sits the mother Mary with her child Jesus, receiving worshippers. Beyond the pillars is seen the blue sky veiled with fleecy clouds. A tiny cloud has floated within the enclosure, bearing two winged cherubs, who hold a cross between them, hovering over the group below.

The company of worshippers kneel on the tessellated pavement: we see from their dress that they are wealthy Venetians of the sixteenth century. It is the family group of a certain Jacopo Pesaro, who was at that time bishop of Paphos. He is known by the familiar nickname of "Baffo," and played an important part in Venetian history.

When the Venetians went forth in the New Crusade to attack the Turks, Pesaro or "Baffo" was the commander of the galleys sent by the Borgia pope Alexander VI. The expedition being successful, the bishop wished to show his gratitude for the divine favor. Accordingly, in the course of time, he ordered this picture as a thank-offering commemorative of his victory. He comes with his kinsman Benedetto and other members of his family to consecrate the standards taken from the enemy.

The bishop himself has the most prominent place among the worshippers at the foot of the throne steps, while Benedetto, with a group behind him, kneels opposite. The victorious commander is accompanied by St. George, who carries the banner inscribed with the papal arms and the Pesaro escutcheon. He leads forward two Turkish captives to whom he turns to speak. St. George was a warrior saint, and being besides the patron of Venice his appearance in this capacity is very appropriate here.

There are other saints to lend their august presence to the ceremony. As the picture was to be given to a church dedicated to the Franciscan friars or "Frari," two of the most celebrated members of this order are represented. They are St. Francis, the founder, and St. Anthony, of Padua, the great preacher, and they stand in the habits of their order beside the throne. Midway on the steps St. Peter is seated reading a book from which he turns to look down upon Jacopo. The key, which is the symbol of his authority in the church, stands on the step below. The saints, we see, form a connecting link between the exalted height of the Madonna and Child and the worshippers. St. Peter introduces the bishop, and St. Francis seems to ask favor for the group with Benedetto.

The scene is full of pomp and grandeur. The superb architecture of the temple, the rich draperies of the sacred group, the splendid dresses of the worshippers, the red and gold banner, all contribute to the impression of magnificence which the picture conveys. The colossal scale of the composition gives us an exhilarating sense of spaciousness. The color harmony is described as glorious.

Though the bishop of Paphos comes to render thanks, his attitude is far from humble. There are no bowed heads in the kneeling company. These proud Pesari all hold themselves erect in conscious self-importance. It is as if they were taking part in some pageant. Only the face of the youth in the corner relaxes from dignified impassivity and looks wistfully out at us.

The Madonna leans graciously from her high throne and looks into the face of the bishop. She, too, has the proud aspect and demeanor which these haughty Venetians would demand of one whom they were to honor. Her splendid vitality is what impresses us most forcibly. The child is a merry little fellow who does not concern himself at all with the ceremony. He has caught up his mother's veil in the left hand, drawing it over his head as if in a game of hide and seek with St. Francis. The little foot is kicked out playfully as he looks down into the good saint's face.

Let us consider a moment the skill with which Titian has united the various parts of his picture. The canvas was of an awkward shape, being of so great height. To fill the space proportionately, the Virgin's throne is placed at a height which divides the picture. The little cloud-borne cherubs break the otherwise undue length of the temple pillars. The composition of the group is outlined in a rather odd-shaped triangle. All its main lines flow diagonally toward a focus in the face of the Virgin, who is of course the dominant figure in the company.

Notice the continuous line extending from the top to the bottom of the group. The folds of the Madonna's drapery are ingeniously carried on in the rich velvet throne hanging; and St. Peter's yellow mantle falls well below, where the bishop's robe takes up the lines and carries them to the pavement. There is a veritable cascade of draperies flowing diagonally through the centre of the picture. The staff of the banner describes a line cutting this main diagonal at exactly the same angle, and thus avoiding any one-sided effect in the picture. In the right of the composition the outline of the Christchild's figure, the arm of St. Francis, and the stiff robe of Benedetto make a series of lines which enclose the triangle on that side.

The critic Ruskin has enunciated a set of laws of composition nearly all of which find illustration in this painting.[26] *Principality* is well exemplified in the prominence of the Virgin's position and the flow of the lines toward her. *Repetition*, *Contrast*, and *Continuity*, are seen in the drawing of the compositional lines, as has been indicated. Finally, the picture is perfect in *Unity*, which is the result of masterly composition, its many diverse parts being bound closely together to form a harmonious whole.

XV

ST. JOHN THE BAPTIST

St. John the Baptist was the cousin of Jesus, and was the elder of the two by about six months. Before his birth the angel Gabriel appeared to his father, Zacharias, and predicted for the coming child a great mission as a prophet. His special work was to prepare the way for the advent of the Messiah.

Zacharias was a priest and a good man, and both he and his wife Elizabeth were deeply impressed with the angel's message. Not long after, their cousin Mary came from Nazareth to bring them news of the wonderful babe Jesus promised her by the same angel. He was to be the Messiah whom John was to proclaim. The two women talked earnestly together of the future of their children, and no doubt planned to do all in their power to further the angel's prediction. The time came when all these strange prophecies were fulfilled. As John grew to manhood he showed himself quite different from other men. He took up his abode in the wilderness, where he lived almost as a hermit. His raiment was of camel's hair fastened about him with a leathern girdle; his food was locusts and wild honey. At length "the word of God came unto him," and he began to go about the country preaching. His speech was as simple and rugged as his manner of life. He boldly denounced the Pharisees and Sadducees as "a generation of vipers," and warned sinners "to flee from the wrath to come." The burden of all his sermons was, "Repent, for the kingdom of heaven is at hand."

The fame of his preaching reached Jerusalem, and the Jews sent priests and Levites to ask him, "Who art thou?' His reply was in the mystic language of the old Hebrew prophet Isaiah, "I am the Voice of one crying in the wilderness, Make straight the way of the Lord."

It was a part of John's work to baptize his converts in the river Jordan. He explained, however, that this baptism by water was only a symbol of the spiritual baptism which they were to receive at the hands of the coming: Messiah. "One mightier than I cometh," he said, "the latchet of whose shoes I am not worthy to unloose: he shall baptize you with the Holy Ghost and with fire."[27]

At last Jesus himself sought to be baptized by John. The Baptist protested his unworthiness, but Jesus insisted, and the ceremony was performed. And "it came to pass that ... the heaven was opened, and the Holy Ghost descended in a bodily shape like a dove upon him, and a voice came from heaven, which said, Thou art my beloved son; in thee I am well pleased."[28] This was the promised sign by which John knew Jesus as the Messiah, and he straightway proclaimed him to his disciples.

His life work was now consummated, but he was not permitted to see the fruits of his labors. For his open denunciation of King Herod he was cast into prison, and was soon after beheaded.

In our picture St. John stands in a mountain glen preaching. As his glance is directed out of the picture it is as if his audience were in front, and we among their number. His pointing finger seems to single out some one to whom he directs attention, and we know well who it is. This must be that day when seeing Jesus approach the prophet exclaimed, "Behold the Lamb of God which taketh away the sin of the world. This is he of whom I said, After me cometh a man which is preferred before me; for he was before me."[29] The lamb which lies on the ground beside him is the outward symbol of his words. The slender reed cross he carries is an emblem of his mission as the prophet of the crucified one.

From head to feet the Baptist impresses us with his muscular power. There is no hint of fastings and vigils in this strong athletic figure. Here, as elsewhere. Titian will have nothing of that piety which is associated with a delicate and puny physique. He is the art apostle of that "muscular Christianity" of which Charles Kingsley used to preach. The Baptist's skin is bronzed and weather-beaten from his active out-of-door life. Yet the face shows the stern and sombre character of the prophet. There are traces of suffering in the expression, as of one who mourns profoundly the evil in the world. Something of the fanatic gleams in the eyes, and the effect is heightened by the wild masses of unkempt hair which frame the countenance.

Nature too seems to be in a somewhat wild and sombre mood in this spot. A dark bank rises abruptly at the side, and St. John stands in its shadow, just under a tuft of coarse grass and bushes jutting from its upper edge. The sky is overcast with clouds. A narrow stream falls over a rocky bed, and in the distance slender trees lift their feathery branches in the air. In Titian's time landscape painting had not developed into an independent art, but was an important part of figure compositions. Our painter always took great pains with his landscapes, making them harmonize, as does this, with the character of the figures.

The picture reminds us of the St. Christopher which we have examined, being, like it, a study direct from the life of some athletic model. Yet here we see to better advantage Titian's work in modelling the nude figure. We can understand that one reason why he could make a draped figure so lifelike was because he studied the anatomy of the human body in undraped models. The figure here stands out almost as if it were done in sculpture.

XVI

PORTRAIT OF TITIAN

Probably no other painter in the world's history was ever granted so long a life in which to develop his art as was Titian. He was a mere boy when he began to paint, and he was still busy with his brush when stricken with plague at the age of ninety-nine.

The years between were full of activity, and every decade was marked by some specially notable work as by a golden milestone. The Assumption of the Virgin was painted at the age of forty, the Pesaro Madonna at fifty, the Presentation of the Virgin in his early sixties, the portrait of Philip II. at about seventy, and St. John the Baptist at eighty. How interesting it would be if we could have a portrait of the man himself painted at each decade!

Titian, however, seems to have been quite lacking in personal vanity. Though a handsome and distinguished-looking man, a fine subject for a portrait, he seldom painted his own likeness. We value the more the fine portrait of our frontispiece painted at the age of eighty-five. The years have dealt so gently with him that we may still call him a handsome man. Yet the face has the shrunken look of old age, there are deep hollows about the eyes, and the features are sharpened under the withered skin. There is an expression which seems almost like awe in the eyes. The painter gazes absently into space as if piercing beyond the veil which separates this world from the next. The mood does not seem to be one of reminiscence, but rather of grave anticipation.

As we study the face we are interested to read in it what we know of the man's character and history. Titian was, as we have seen, a man who enjoyed very much the good things of life, and passed most of his days in luxurious surroundings. He was thoroughly a man of the world, at ease in the society of princes and noblemen, and a princely host in his own house. Our portrait shows that his courtly bearing did not fail him in his old age: we can fancy the ceremonious courtesy of his manner. The figure is extended well below the waist, perhaps that we may see how erect the old man is.

Titian, too, had not a little taste for literature and the society of the learned. His fine high brow and keen eyes are sufficient evidence that he was a man of intellect. That he was a fond father we have no doubt, and we like to trace the lines of kindliness in the fine old face.

Age cannot quench the old man's ardor for his art. The brush is still his familiar companion, and will go with him to the end. He holds it here in his right hand, in the attitude of a painter pausing to get the effect of his work. It may be from this that he would have us think that his glance is directed toward his canvas. In that case, the serious expression would indicate that the subject is a solemn one, perhaps the Ecce Homo, or the Pieta, which he painted in his later years.

We see that his hand had not lost its cunning in summoning before us the real presence of a sitter, and that he could paint his own likeness as readily as that of another. The portrait shows us the best elements in a man of a many-sided nature. This is Titian the master, whom the world honors as one of the greatest of his kind.

NOTES ON WORKS

THE DUCHESS OF URBINO.
(In the Uffizi Gallery, Florence)

This portrait of the Duchess of Urbino from the Uffizi must not be confused with the portrait of the Duchess in the Pitti Palace. The sitter here is Eleonora Gonzaga, Duchess of Urbino, and the portrait was painted somewhere between the years 1536 and 1538 at a period when the master's art had ripened almost to the point of its highest achievement.

LA BELLA
(In the Pitti Palace, Florence)

This wonderful example of Titian's portrait painting may be seen in the Pitti Palace to-day, and was probably commissioned by the Duke of Urbino somewhere about the year 1536. It will be noticed by students of Titian that the model for this portrait appears in some of the master's pictures as Venus.

THE ENTOMBMENT
(In the Louvre)

This world-famous canvas hangs in the Salon Carré of the Louvre. It is considered to be one of the masterpieces among the religious subjects painted by the great Venetian artist.

THE HOLY FAMILY
(In the Uffizi Gallery, Florence)

Sometimes known as the Virgin with the Holy Child and Saints. Here we find Titian dealing with a religious subject with the restraint, dignity, and sense of beauty that proclaim him a master among painters. The motherly love of the Virgin, the solicitude of St. Joseph on the right, and the childish innocence of the two children are most effectively expressed and contrasted. The picture may be seen in the Uffizi Gallery.

FOOTNOTES

1. See notes on Titian in Vasari's *Lives of the Painters*, edited by E. H. and E. W. Blashfield and A. A. Hopkins.

2. Notes on Titian in Vasari's *Lives of the Painters*, by E. H. and E. W. Blashfield and A. A. Hopkins.

3. Claude Phillips.

4. Compiled from the Index to *Titian: His Life and Times*, by Crowe and Cavalcaselle.

5. As the various so-called portraits of Vesalius are said to have little in common upon which to base a resemblance, one is almost tempted to set up a theory that this portrait may be that of the great anatomist.

6. 1 Samuel, chapter i., verses 11, 24-28.

7. *The Golden Legend*, in Caxton's translation, edited by F. S. Ellis (Temple Classics, vol. v., pp. 101, 102). The story is retold in Mrs. Jameson's *Legends of the Madonna*, p. 197.

8. For instance, Lavinia, Flora, and the Man with the Glove.

9. See the Acts of the Apostles, chapters vi. and vii.

10. The lives of St. Jerome and St. George are related in detail in *The Golden Legend*. See Caxton's translation edited by F.S. Ellis (Temple Classics), vol. v., pages 199-208, for St. Jerome, vol. iii., pages 125-134, for St. George. Mrs. Jameson's *Sacred and Legendary Art* contains condensed accounts of the same two saints. See page 280 for St. Jerome and page 391 for St. George.

11. See the story as related in Mrs. Jameson's *Sacred and Legendary Art*, page 433, and in H.E. Scudder's *Book of Legends*.

12. Claude Phillips.

13. Matthew, chapter xxii., verses 34-40.

14. Others are the Venus of the Uffizi Gallery, Florence, and the Girl in the Fur Cloak in the Belvedere, Vienna.

15. In the later Venetian art, as in the pictures by Veronese, we see more elaborate costumes.

16. See Book VII. in Henry King's translation, from which the quotations here are drawn. The same story is delightfully modernized in Hawthorne's *Tanglewood Tales* and Kingsley's *Greek Heroes*.

17. See the volume on *Greek Sculpture* in the Riverside Art Series, chap. xiii.

18. From *Gareth and Lynette*.

19. From *Guinevere*.

20. This analysis of Mary's character is suggested in the Introduction to Mrs. Jameson's *Legends of the Madonna*, p. 28.

21. See the volume on *Murillo* in the Riverside Art Series, Chapter I.

22. See *The Golden Legend*, in Caxton's translation, edited by F. S. Ellis (Temple Classics), vol. iv., pages 238, 239, 245.

23. Mrs. Jameson in *Sacred and Legendary Art*, page 74.

24. This feature of the picture is pointed out by John Van Dyke in his notes on Closson's engraving of the subject.

25. It should be remembered that a portion of Elizabeth's reign (1538-1603) fell within Titian's lifetime.

26. See *Elements of Drawing*, Lecture III.

27. Luke, chapter iii., verse 6.

28. Luke, chapter iii., verses 21, 22.

29. John, chapter i., verses 29-30.

CRESCENT MOON PUBLISHING

web: www.crmoon.com e-mail: cresmopub@yahoo.co.uk

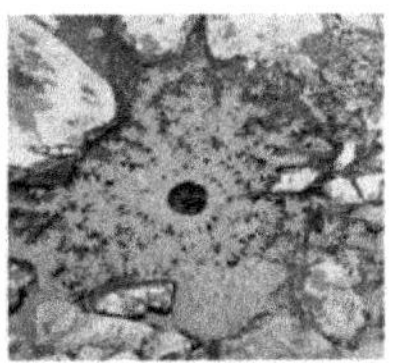

ARTS, PAINTING, SCULPTURE

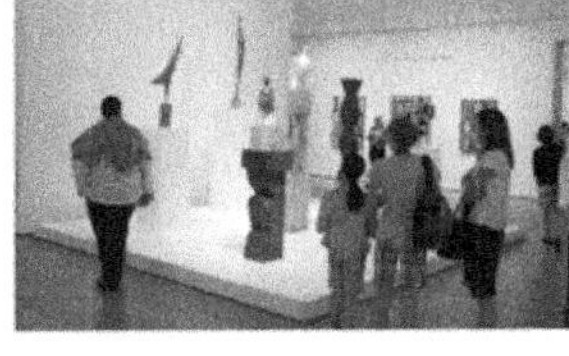

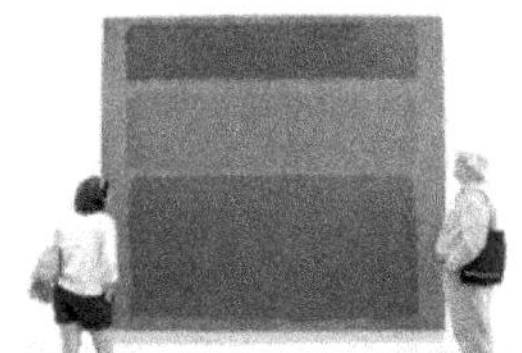

The Art of Andy Goldsworthy
Andy Goldsworthy: Touching Nature
Andy Goldsworthy in Close-Up
Andy Goldsworthy: Pocket Guide
Andy Goldsworthy In America
Land Art: A Complete Guide
The Art of Richard Long
Richard Long: Pocket Guide
Land Art In the UK
Land Art in Close-Up
Land Art In the U.S.A.
Land Art: Pocket Guide
Installation Art in Close-Up
Minimal Art and Artists In the 1960s and After
Colourfield Painting
Land Art DVD, TV documentary
Andy Goldsworthy DVD, TV documentary
The Erotic Object: Sexuality in Sculpture From Prehistory to the Present Day
Sex in Art: Pornography and Pleasure in Painting and Sculpture
Postwar Art
Sacred Gardens: The Garden in Myth, Religion and Art
Glorification: Religious Abstraction in Renaissance and 20th Century Art
Early Netherlandish Painting
Leonardo da Vinci
Piero della Francesca
Giovanni Bellini
Fra Angelico: Art and Religion in the Renaissance
Mark Rothko: The Art of Transcendence
Frank Stella: American Abstract Artist
Jasper Johns
Brice Marden
Alison Wilding: The Embrace of Sculpture
Vincent van Gogh: Visionary Landscapes
Eric Gill: Nuptials of God
Constantin Brancusi: Sculpting the Essence of Things
Max Beckmann
Caravaggio
Gustave Moreau
Egon Schiele: Sex and Death In Purple Stockings
Delizioso Fotografico Fervore: Works In Process 1
Sacro Cuore: Works In Process 2
The Light Eternal: J.M.W. Turner
The Madonna Glorified: Karen Arthurs

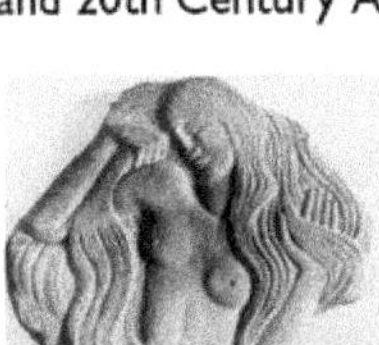

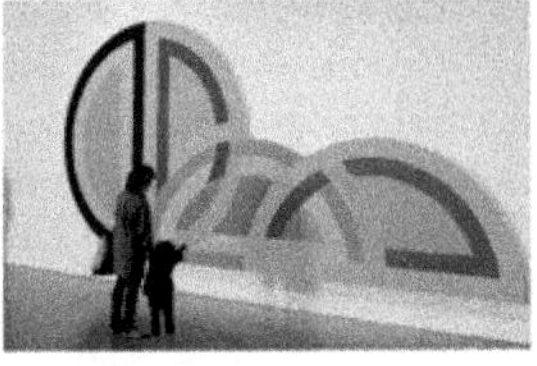

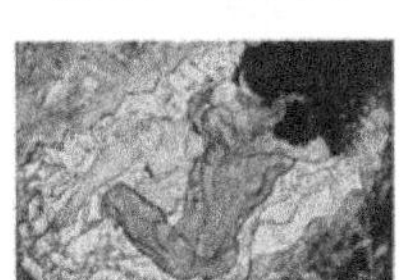

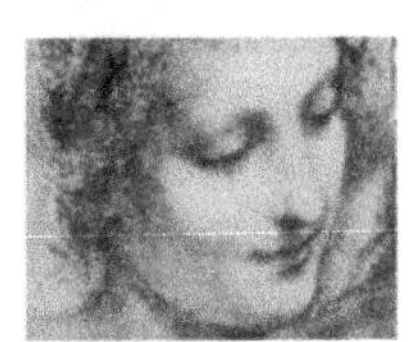

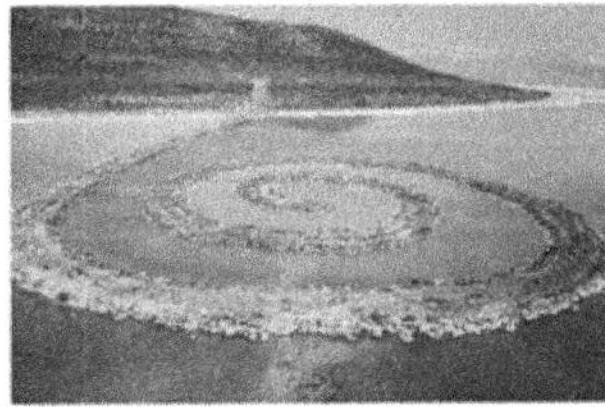

LITERATURE

J.R.R. Tolkien: The Books, The Films, The Whole Cultural Phenomenon
J.R.R. Tolkien: Pocket Guide
Tolkien's Heroic Quest
The *Earthsea* Books of Ursula Le Guin
Beauties, Beasts and Enchantment: Classic French Fairy Tales
German Popular Stories by the Brothers Grimm
Philip Pullman and *His Dark Materials*
Sexing Hardy: Thomas Hardy and Feminism
Thomas Hardy's *Tess of the d'Urbervilles*
Thomas Hardy's *Jude the Obscure*
Thomas Hardy: The Tragic Novels
Love and Tragedy: Thomas Hardy
The Poetry of Landscape in Hardy
Wessex Revisited: Thomas Hardy and John Cowper Powys
Wolfgang Iser: Essays and Interviews
Petrarch, Dante and the Troubadours
Maurice Sendak and the Art of Children's Book Illustration
Andrea Dworkin
Cixous, Irigaray, Kristeva: The *Jouissance* of French Feminism
Julia Kristeva: Art, Love, Melancholy, Philosophy, Semiotics and Psychoanalysis
Hélene Cixous I Love You: The *Jouissance* of Writing
Luce Irigaray: Lips, Kissing, and the Politics of Sexual Difference
Peter Redgrove: Here Comes the Flood
Peter Redgrove: Sex-Magic-Poetry-Cornwall
Lawrence Durrell: Between Love and Death, East and West
Love, Culture & Poetry: Lawrence Durrell
Cavafy: Anatomy of a Soul
German Romantic Poetry: Goethe, Novalis, Heine, Hölderlin
Feminism and Shakespeare
Shakespeare: Love, Poetry & Magic
The Passion of D.H. Lawrence
D.H. Lawrence: Symbolic Landscapes
D.H. Lawrence: Infinite Sensual Violence
Rimbaud: Arthur Rimbaud and the Magic of Poetry
The Ecstasies of John Cowper Powys
Sensualism and Mythology: The Wessex Novels of John Cowper Powys
Amorous Life: John Cowper Powys and the Manifestation of Affectivity (H.W. Fawkner)
Postmodern Powys: New Essays on John Cowper Powys (Joe Boulter)
Rethinking Powys: Critical Essays on John Cowper Powys
Paul Bowles & Bernardo Bertolucci
Rainer Maria Rilke
Joseph Conrad: *Heart of Darkness*
In the Dim Void: Samuel Beckett
Samuel Beckett Goes into the Silence
André Gide: Fiction and Fervour
Jackie Collins and the Blockbuster Novel
Blinded By Her Light: The Love-Poetry of Robert Graves
The Passion of Colours: Travels In Mediterranean Lands
Poetic Forms

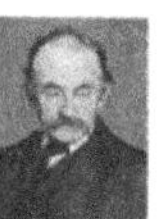
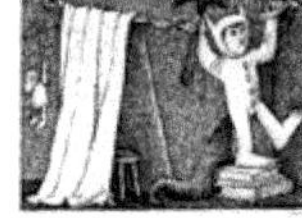
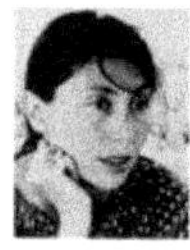
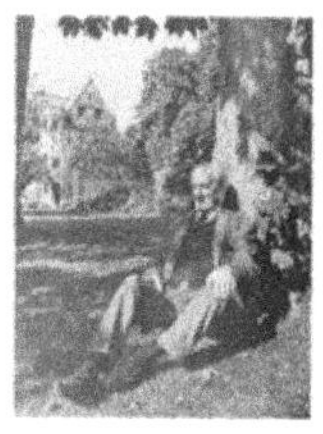
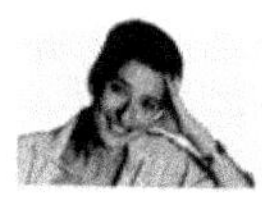
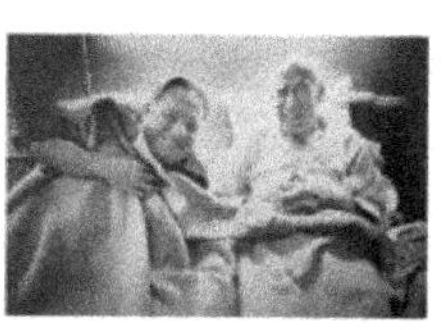
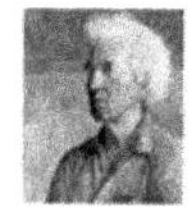
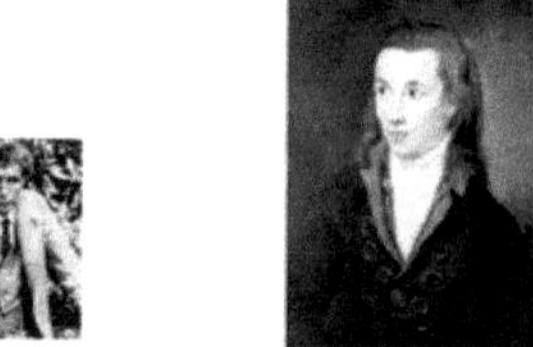

POETRY

Ursula Le Guin: Walking In Cornwall
Peter Redgrove: Here Comes The Flood
Peter Redgrove: Sex-Magic-Poetry-Cornwall
Dante: Selections From the Vita Nuova
Petrarch, Dante and the Troubadours
William Shakespeare: Sonnets
William Shakespeare: Complete Poems
Blinded By Her Light: The Love-Poetry of Robert Graves
Emily Dickinson: Selected Poems
Emily Brontë: Poems
Thomas Hardy: Selected Poems
Percy Bysshe Shelley: Poems
John Keats: Selected Poems
Joh n Keats: Poems of 1820
D.H. Lawrence: Selected Poems
Edmund Spenser: Poems
Edmund Spenser: Amoretti
John Donne: Poems
Henry Vaughan: Poems
Sir Thomas Wyatt: Poems
Robert Herrick: Selected Poems
Rilke: Space, Essence and Angels in the Poetry of Rainer Maria Rilke
Rainer Maria Rilke: Selected Poems
Friedrich Hölderlin: Selected Poems
Arseny Tarkovsky: Selected Poems
Arthur Rimbaud: Selected Poems
Arthur Rimbaud: A Season in Hell
Arthur Rimbaud and the Magic of Poetry
Novalis: Hymns To the Night
German Romantic Poetry
Paul Verlaine: Selected Poems
Elizaethan Sonnet Cycles
D.J. Enright: By-Blows
Jeremy Reed: Brigitte's Blue Heart
Jeremy Reed: Claudia Schiffer's Red Shoes
Gorgeous Little Orpheus
Radiance: New Poems
Crescent Moon Book of Nature Poetry
Crescent Moon Book of Love Poetry
Crescent Moon Book of Mystical Poetry
Crescent Moon Book of Elizabethan Love Poetry
Crescent Moon Book of Metaphysical Poetry
Crescent Moon Book of Romantic Poetry
Pagan America: New American Poetry

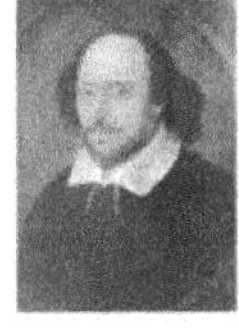
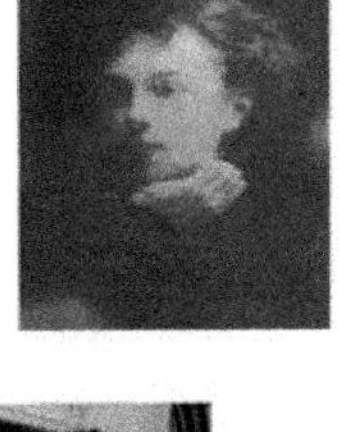
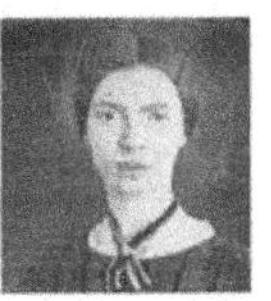
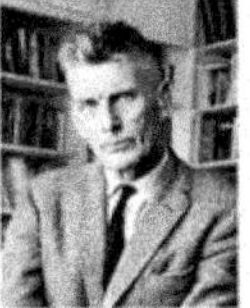
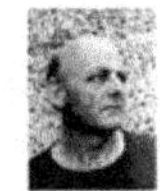
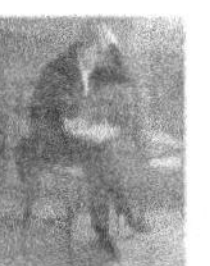
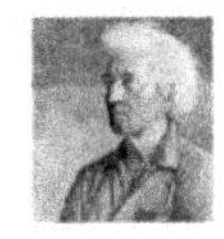
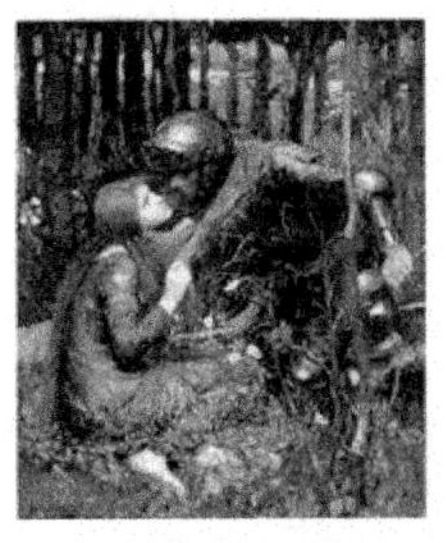
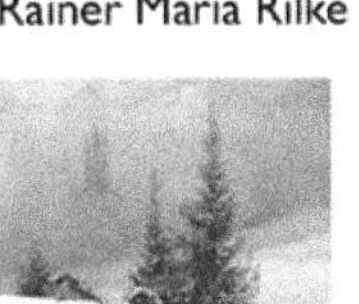
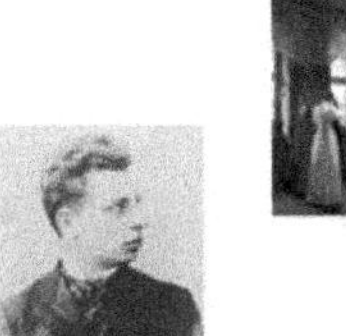
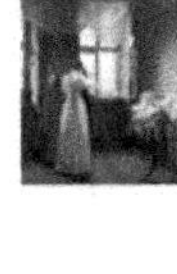
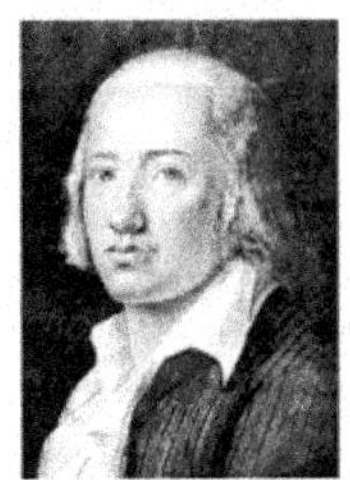
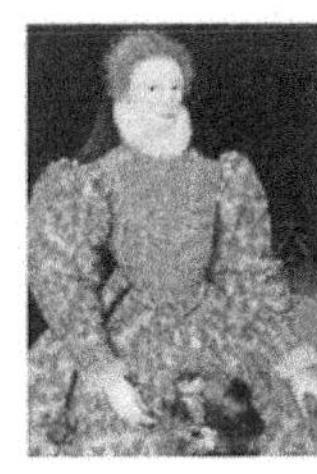

MEDIA, CINEMA, FEMINISM and CULTURAL STUDIES

J.R.R. Tolkien: The Books, The Films, The Whole Cultural Phenomenon
J.R.R. Tolkien: Pocket Guide
The *Lord of the Rings* Movies: Pocket Guide
The Cinema of Hayao Miyazaki
Hayao Miyazaki: *Princess Mononoke*: Pocket Movie Guide
Hayao Miyazaki: *Spirited Away*: Pocket Movie Guide
Tim Burton : Hallowe'en For Hollywood
Ken Russell
Ken Russell: *Tommy*: Pocket Movie Guide
The Ghost Dance: The Origins of Religion
The Peyote Cult

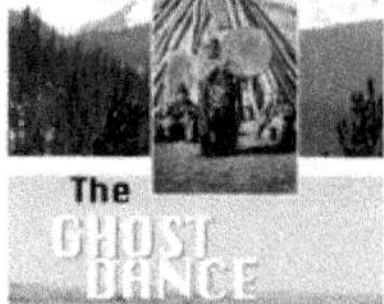

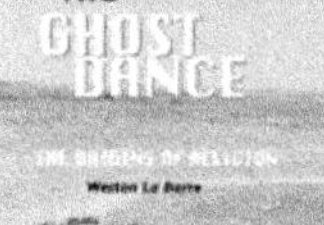

Cixous, Irigaray, Kristeva: The *Jouissance* of French Feminism
Julia Kristeva: Art, Love, Melancholy, Philosophy, Semiotics and Psychoanalysis
Luce Irigaray: Lips, Kissing, and the Politics of Sexual Difference
Hélene Cixous I Love You: The *Jouissance* of Writing
Andrea Dworkin
'Cosmo Woman': The World of Women's Magazines
Women in Pop Music
HomeGround: The Kate Bush Anthology

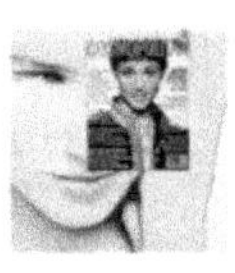

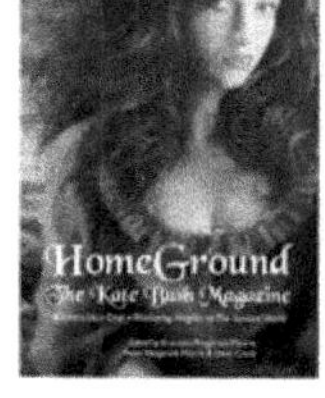

Discovering the Goddess (Geoffrey Ashe)
The Poetry of Cinema
The Sacred Cinema of Andrei Tarkovsky
Andrei Tarkovsky: Pocket Guide
Andrei Tarkovsky: *Mirror*: Pocket Movie Guide
Andrei Tarkovsky: *The Sacrifice*: Pocket Movie Guide
Walerian Borowczyk: Cinema of Erotic Dreams
Jean-Luc Godard: The Passion of Cinema

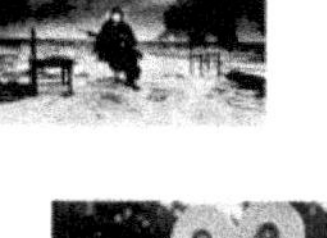

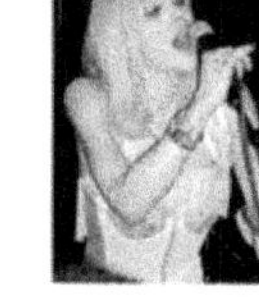

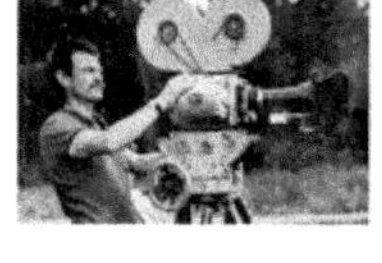

Jean-Luc Godard: *Hail Mary*: Pocket Movie Guide
Jean-Luc Godard: *Contempt*: Pocket Movie Guide
Jean-Luc Godard: *Pierrot le Fou*: Pocket Movie Guide
John Hughes and Eighties Cinema
Ferris Bueller's Day Off: Pocket Movie Guide
Jean-Luc Godard: Pocket Guide
The Cinema of Richard Linklater

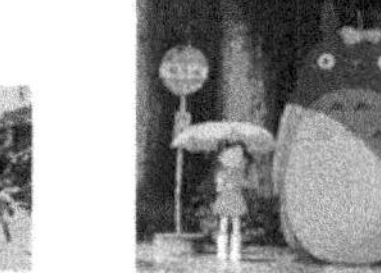

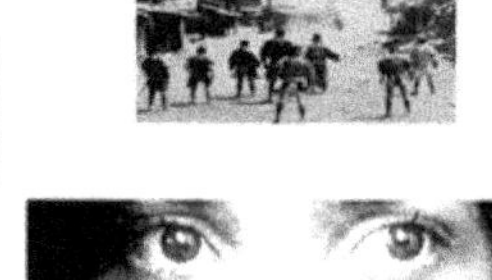

Liv Tyler: Star In Ascendance
Blade Runner and the Films of Philip K. Dick
Paul Bowles and Bernardo Bertolucci
Media Hell: Radio, TV and the Press
An Open Letter to the BBC
Detonation Britain: Nuclear War in the UK

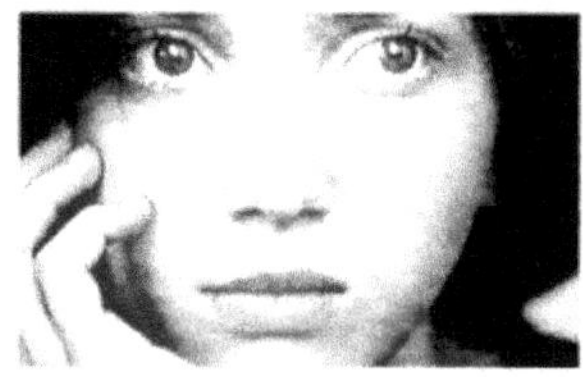

Feminism and Shakespeare
Wild Zones: Pornography, Art and Feminism
Sex in Art: Pornography and Pleasure in Painting and Sculpture
Sexing Hardy: Thomas Hardy and Feminism

The Light Eternal is a model monograph, an exemplary job. The subject matter of the book is beautifully organised and dead on beam. (Lawrence Durrell)

It is amazing for me to see my work treated with such passion and respect. (Andrea Dworkin)

CRESCENT MOON PUBLISHING
P.O. Box 1312, Maidstone, Kent, ME14 5XU, Great Britain. www.crmoon.com

cresmopub@yahoo.co.uk www.crescentmoon.org.uk

www.ingramcontent.com/pod-product-compliance
Ingram Content Group UK Ltd.
Pitfield, Milton Keynes, MK11 3LW, UK
UKHW020427250726
13967UKWH00007B/2835

9 781861 716088